Family Activities and Positive Behavior

202 Engaging Ideas for Building Stronger Relationships and Fostering Good Habits in Children

Table of Contents

Part 1: Family Activities

101 Fun Ideas, Games, and Crafts to Strengthen Parent-Child Relationships

Introduction

Spending quality time with family is crucial and adds meaning to our lives. Unfortunately, with busy schedules and daily routines, we often forget to make time for our loved ones. So, developing activities to bond the family and create lasting memories becomes vital. This comprehensive guide shares some fun ideas for family activities to keep everyone entertained.

Spending quality time with family strengthens relationships. These bonds create and nurture the relationship between family members, making them feel close to one another. Taking part in activities together is an excellent way to do this. This book also includes ideas for screen-free games and projects so you can talk, laugh, and share stories as a family. It also covers tasks that encourage teamwork and create a sense of unity in the family.

In today's world, screens dominate our lives, and it's no secret that excessive screen time can damage the bond between family members. While technology can be helpful, taking a break from screens and finding other ways to spend quality time together is vital. Hidden in the pages of this book are outdoor adventure ideas that can help the family reconnect with nature.

Creative souls will get to unleash their inner artists when they explore the art and craft ideas included in this book. Game night can also be exciting with some interesting twists, which will be discussed in later chapters. Cooking together is a great way to bond and learn from each other. So, why not put on aprons and get everyone to spend time in the kitchen? Baking is another activity that will bring the family together with a yummy result.

Storytelling is a powerful tool used for centuries as an ancient form of entertainment. This guide will teach you to share stories and make tales together, creating a magical atmosphere. Fitness activities have also been added for those who want to stay active together as a family. Finally, explore some ideas for day trips you can take together and create wonderful, lasting memories with your loved ones. This book also includes ideas for family traditions you can start and cherish forever.

Spending quality time with your family should be a smooth process. With this guide, you will find many fun activities the whole family can enjoy together. Regardless of where you are or what you're doing, setting aside some time for your family is essential. After all, the family is all we have when it comes down to it. So why not use this book as a starting point and create some fantastic memories together? Happy bonding!

Chapter 1: The Importance of Building Bonds

To foster strong, positive relationships between parents and their children, the time you spend together has to be of high quality. Whether enjoying a stroll around the park or playing board games together, engaging in fun activities with your family is a sure way to build lasting bonds. This chapter examines the importance of precious quality family time and its impact on parent-child relationships, how flexibility in activities can lead to greater connection and the educational benefits of engaging in fun activities together. You'll also find some tips and tricks on fostering a stronger, more meaningful relationship between parents and their children.

Quality Time and Its Impact on Parent-Child Relationships

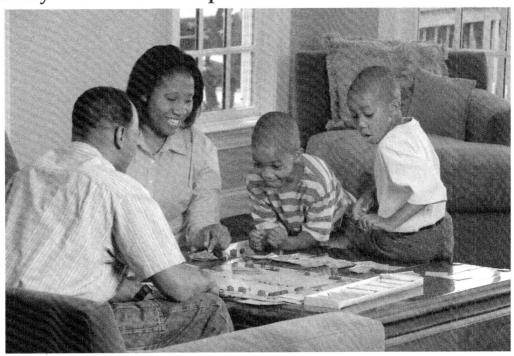

Spending quality time with your children can help you build a healthy parent-child relationship.
https://unsplash.com/photos/VJVsEnR_vNE?utm_source=unsplash&utm_medium=referral&utm_content=creditShareLink

Spending dedicated quality time with your child is essential to building a strong and healthy parent-child relationship. Quality time means giving undivided attention to your family, communicating clearly, listening actively, participating in activities together, and creating precious memories. This section will explore the importance of quality time, explain how it impacts parent-child relationships, and suggest ways to incorporate it into your daily routine.

Importance of Quality Time

Quality time is one of the keys to building a close, supportive, and long-lasting relationship with your child. Children feel loved and valued when they receive attention and affection from their parents. When parents devote time to their children, they establish a strong bond and trust that can improve communication, reduce negative behavior, and promote emotional and social development. In addition, quality time builds confidence, self-esteem, and a sense of security in children, making them better able to cope with challenges and stress in the future.

Impact of Quality Time on Parent-Child Relationships

Spending regular quality time with your child helps you understand your child's needs, interests, strengths, and weaknesses. It deepens your connection and trust with your child, leading to better communication, problem-solving, and decision-making. Research has shown that children with quality time with their parents are less likely to experience depression, anxiety, and behavioral problems. In addition, they are more likely to perform better academically, have better social skills, and be less likely to engage in risky behaviors, such as drug and alcohol abuse.

Ways to Incorporate Quality Time into Your Daily Routine

You don't have to spend hours to provide quality time for your child. Instead, you can incorporate quality time into your daily routine, even with a busy schedule. Here are some ideas:

- **Create a Family Ritual**. For example, have dinner together every night, read a book before bedtime, or go on a weekend outing.
- **Turn Off Distractions**. Be fully present when spending time with your child. Turn off your phone, the TV, or anything distracting.
- **Ask Open-Ended Questions**. Encourage conversation by asking open-ended questions like "What was the best part of your day?" or "Tell me about your favorite hobby."
- **Participate in Your Child's Interests**. Join your child in activities that interest them, such as playing board games, drawing, or sports.
- **Plan One-on-One Time**: Plan special activities or outings with each child. It could be as simple as going for a walk or baking cookies.

Quality Time Is Not Just for Children

Quality time is not just for children but for parents, too. Spending time with your child can help you relax, reduce stress, boost your mood, and improve your mental health. It is also an opportunity to learn from your child, have fun, and create memories that will last a lifetime. As a parent, it can be easy to put yourself last, but remember, self-care is as important as taking care of your child. Make sure you have time to recharge, reflect, and appreciate the joys of parenting.

Spending quality time with your child is a valuable investment in your child's life and well-being. It is an opportunity to build a solid and lasting parent-child relationship, promote your child's emotional and social development, and create precious memories. Remember, quality time does not have to be complicated or expensive. It can be as simple as reading a book or having a conversation. Make time for your child, turn off distractions, and enjoy each other's company. Your child will thank you for it.

The Power of Flexibility in Parent-Child Relationships

Parenting can be challenging and sometimes frustrating, especially when we do not have all the answers. But we need to understand that our children are not robots. Instead, they are unique individuals with their own particular personalities, strengths, and weaknesses. Therefore, adopting a flexible parenting style that can adapt to your children's different needs and developmental stages is crucial. This section will explore the power of flexibility in parent-child relationships and its impact on your children's overall well-being.

Accepting your child's individuality is a big step in exercising flexibility.
https://pixabay.com/id/photos/gadis-ibu-anak-perempuan-2480361/

The first step to implementing flexibility is understanding and accepting our child's individuality. Every child has a different temperament, learning style, and pace. So, a one-size-fits-all approach is not going to work. Instead, we should focus on adapting our parenting to fit each child's individual needs. By embracing your child's individuality, you create a nurturing environment that supports their emotional and psychological development.

Scientific Benefits of Engaging in Fun Activities with the Family

Doing fun activities as a family has many scientific benefits.
https://www.pexels.com/photo/family-playing-charades-at-bonfire-in-garden-5638830/

Family time is crucial in today's fast-paced world, where everyone is busy. Spending quality time with family strengthens bonds and has numerous benefits, such as reducing stress levels, boosting self-esteem, and improving mental health. What's even more interesting is engaging in fun activities as a family can lead to significant scientific benefits that impact our lives in both short-term and long-term ways. Let's explore some of these surprising scientific benefits of engaging in fun activities with family:

- **Improved Cognitive Functioning:** Family fun activities involving games, sports, or puzzles can enhance cognitive processes, such as memory, reasoning, and problem-solving skills. Studies reveal that family fun activities boost creativity and improve mental resilience, enhancing brain connectivity and overall cognitive functioning.

- **Better Emotional Stability:** Engaging in fun activities with family regulates mood and reduces stress levels. Family fun time develops a sense of belonging and emotional security, contributing to stable emotional health. In addition, studies suggest that family fun time provides emotional support and strengthens empathy and compassion in children.

- **Healthy Physical Development:** Activities, such as outdoor sports, hiking, or cycling all improve physical development and lead to healthier lifestyles. Engaging in fun physical activities with family promotes physical exercise, leading to better cardiovascular health, stronger bones, enhanced muscle strength, and a better immune system.

- **Improved Communication Skills:** Engaging in family activities opens up opportunities for family members to communicate and interact in a relaxed, non-judgmental setting. This develops better communication skills, leading to enhanced social functioning and improved relational dynamics within the family.

- **Long-Term Social Benefits:** Engaging in fun activities has long-term social benefits too. Positive family experiences lead to better academic performance, improved social functioning, and improved relationships with peers later in their lives.

Engaging in fun activities with family strengthens family bonds and has several surprising scientific benefits. These benefits impact our lives in both short and long-term ways, contributing to better cognitive functioning, healthier physical development, improved emotional stability, and better communication skills.

Tips for Fostering Family Connections

Family is the most important thing in everyone's life. It's the foundation of our support, love, and care. However, spending quality time with our families with our busy lives and schedules can be challenging. This section will discuss tips that will help you foster stronger family connections, regardless of your busy life.

- **Set Aside Time for Family:** The first step to cultivating family connections is to set aside time for family. No matter how busy your schedule is, prioritize spending time with your loved ones. It can be done by planning family outings, game nights, or simply sitting down for dinner together. When you set aside time for family, you make it clear that they are a priority in your life, which builds more robust connections.

- **Create Shared Experiences:** Shared experiences are a great way to build stronger connections with family members. It can be anything from going on a vacation, taking a cooking class, or simply trying out a new hobby together. The key is finding something you all enjoy, allowing you to get closer over a common interest. It not only creates lasting memories but also strengthens the family bond.

- **Communicate Regularly:** Communication is vital to building strong family connections. Always check in with your family and ask about their day-to-day life. This can be done by simply sending a text or making a quick phone call. By staying connected and engaging in open communication, you can better understand each other's thoughts and feelings, strengthening your relationship.

- **Be Present Now:** Being present is essential when spending time with family. This means putting away distractions like your phone and focusing on the present moment. You can strengthen your bond and create lasting memories by giving your undivided attention.

In conclusion, family connections are essential to our well-being, and it's vital to make an effort to strengthen them. By setting aside time for family, creating shared experiences, communicating regularly, practicing forgiveness, and being present in the moment, you can foster stronger family connections that will last a lifetime. Love and support begin with family, so make the most of it.

Fostering Strong Parent-Child Relationships

Parenting is a tough job, and no one always gets it right. But one of the most important things you can do as a parent is to nurture a positive and secure relationship with your child. A strong parent-child relationship builds the foundation for a happy and fulfilling life for you and your child.

There are many ways to create and maintain a positive and nurturing environment for your child. This section will discuss tips and strategies for fostering a strong and loving parent-child relationship.

Be Open and Honest

Communication is vital to any successful relationship; the parent-child relationship is no exception. When you communicate with your child, listen actively and respond honestly. For example, encourage your child to express their feelings and concerns unreservedly and offer support and guidance when needed. Remember that communication is a two-way street. It would be best to share your thoughts and feelings with your child. Be open, honest, and transparent with your child. They will trust and respect you for it.

Spend Quality Time Together

Spend quality time with your child regularly. This does not have to be a big, elaborate event. Even 15 minutes of one-on-one time each day can make a big difference. During this time, focus on your child and make them feel special. Engage in activities your child enjoys and use this time to connect with them emotionally.

Show Affection and Gratitude

Showing affection and gratitude is another way to nurture a positive parent-child relationship. Express your love, appreciation, and gratitude to your child regularly. Hugs, kisses, and kind words can go a long way in making your child feel secure, loved, and valued.

Set Boundaries and Provide Guidance

As a parent, setting boundaries and advising your child is crucial. This creates a sense of safety and structure for your child and develops a strong sense of right and wrong in them. When setting boundaries, be clear, consistent, and fair. And when providing guidance, do so with love, respect, firmness, and a clear sense of authority.

Nurturing a positive and loving parent-child relationship requires effort and dedication, but the rewards are immeasurable. By communicating openly and honestly, spending quality time together, showing affection and gratitude, setting boundaries, providing guidance, and being a positive role model, you can help your child develop a solid and loving relationship with you that will last a lifetime. The next chapter will explore screen-free activities you can do as a family to foster strong family connections. The home, after all, is where love and support truly begin.

Chapter 2: Screen-Free Activities

With the rise of digital media, it has become increasingly difficult for families to spend quality time together without distractions from screens. When parents and their children are disconnected, a lack of meaningful interaction leads to misunderstandings and potential conflict. Regaining activities that foster face-to-face interaction is vital to improving communication and creating strong bonds within the family.

This chapter discusses the importance of screen-free time and making space for meaningful connections within the family. It outlines activities encouraging parent-child bonding through creative, interactive, and hands-on experiences. The activities featured in this chapter cater to different age groups and interests; everyone can find something they enjoy!

Benefits of Face-to-Face Interaction

Face-to-face interaction with your children can improve communication skills.
https://www.pexels.com/photo/child-hugging-a-woman-face-to-face-7173482/

Most families struggle to prioritize face-to-face interaction over screen time in today's digital age. However, screen time negatively impacts social-emotional development in children. Therefore, families must participate in screen-free activities to promote interpersonal communication and connection. This section explores the benefits of face-to-face interactions and some fun, screen-free activities that families can share.

- **Improved Communication Skills:** Face-to-face conversations allow nonverbal cues and body language to complement spoken words, which is essential for effective communication. By practicing personal interactions, children learn how to read social cues, develop empathy, and express themselves better, setting them up for success in personal and professional relationships.

- **Opportunity to Build Strong Relationships:** Personal interactions help you to develop a deep connection with your loved ones, creating a sense of belonging and unity. Family activities like board games, hiking, and making meals together offer an opportunity to bond over specific interests and shared experiences. These activities create memories that last a lifetime and strengthen familial relationships.

- **Better Mental Health:** According to the American Psychological Association, excessive screen time can lead to health issues, such as sleep deprivation, obesity, and poor academic performance. Conversely, face-to-face interactions affect mental health positively. For example, personal conversations have a calming effect on the brain, promoting positive feelings and reducing stress levels.

- **Improved Attention and Focus Skills:** People who spend less time on screens tend to have better mental focus and attention skills. Screen-free activities like playing sports, creating arts and crafts, or practicing mindfulness exercises facilitate mental de-stress, translating to better performance in school and other activities.

While avoiding technology altogether is impossible, prioritizing face-to-face interactions can bring your family closer, create lasting memories, and promote emotional well-being. Incorporating screen-free activities into your routine can help you strengthen relationships, have fun, and reap the positive benefits of personal interactions. So, it's time to put down the screens and start connecting.

Board Game Nights

Board games are one of the most enjoyable screen-free activities.
https://unsplash.com/photos/NrS53eUKgiE?utm_source=unsplash&utm_medium=referral&utm_content=creditShareLink

Playing board games with friends and family is a fun way to strengthen relationships while enjoying some competitive fun. This section explores some exciting board game night ideas that are screen-free and perfect for families to enjoy together.

Activity 1: Classic Board Games: Nostalgia and Learning in Every Move

Classic board games are a nostalgic way to bring generations together for a night of laughter and competition. These games offer entertainment and valuable learning experiences for players of all ages.

Step-by-Step Instructions:

1. Choose the Game: Select a classic board game like Monopoly, Scrabble, or Clue. Consider the preferences and ages of the players involved.

2. Set Up: Unfold the game board and distribute playing pieces, cards, and accessories. Review the rules together.

3. Take Turns: Begin the game by rolling dice or drawing cards to determine the order of play. Take turns clockwise, following the game's rules.

4. Follow the Rules: Read and follow the rules for each game. Make strategic decisions like buying properties, forming words, or solving mysteries.

5. Engage in Gameplay: Engage in the game, trading properties, forming words, or solving mysteries, depending on the game chosen.

6. Learn and Adapt: Embrace the learning aspect of the game. Monopoly teaches about money management, Scrabble enhances vocabulary, and Clue sharpens deductive reasoning.

7. Finish the Game: Continue playing until a predetermined goal is reached, such as bankruptcy in Monopoly or solving the mystery in Clue.

8. Celebrate the Winner: Congratulate the winner and reflect on the fun moments and strategic moves during the game.

Benefits:

- Multi-generational Bonding: Classic games bridge generation gaps, enabling grandparents, parents, and children to bond over shared experiences.

- Educational: Each game imparts unique skills. Monopoly teaches financial literacy, Scrabble enhances language skills, and Clue boosts critical thinking.

Activity 2: Cooperative Games: Teamwork and Triumph Unite

Cooperative board games foster a sense of unity as players collaborate to overcome challenges. These games teach invaluable teamwork and communication skills.

Step-by-Step Instructions:

1. Select the Game: Choose a cooperative game like Forbidden Island or Pandemic. These games require players to work together to achieve a common goal.
2. Understand the Objective: Familiarize everyone with the game's objective, whether recovering treasures or saving the world from a pandemic.
3. Assign Roles: Assign roles or characters to each player, each with unique abilities contributing to the team's success.
4. Discuss Strategy: Collaborate on a game plan. Share ideas, suggest moves, and consider the best course of action.
5. Take Turns: Follow the game's turn-based structure. Each player makes decisions to advance the team's progress.
6. Utilize Abilities: Make the most of each character's abilities to tackle challenges and obstacles.
7. Communicate Effectively: Constant communication is key. Discuss strategies, potential risks, and cooperative moves.
8. Work Towards Victory: Strive to achieve the game's objective as a team. Adapt and adjust strategies as new challenges arise.
9. Celebrate Victory: Celebrate a team victory with a sense of shared accomplishment, highlighting key contributions from each player.

Benefits:

- Team Bonding: Players develop a strong sense of unity and camaraderie as they work together towards victory.
- Communication Skills: Cooperative games enhance communication and decision-making skills as players must discuss strategies and coordinate actions.

Activity 3: Strategy Games: Unleashing Tactical Brilliance

Strategy board games provide intellectually stimulating experiences that demand critical thinking, planning, and astute decision-making.

Step-by-Step Instructions:

1. Choose the Game: Opt for a strategy game, such as Settlers of Catan, Ticket to Ride, or Risk. These games offer complex challenges.

2. Setup: Set up the game board, distribute resources or cards, and place playing pieces as per the game's instructions.

3. Understand Rules: Familiarize players with the chosen strategy game's rules, victory conditions, and gameplay mechanics.

4. Initial Moves: Make strategic opening moves that set the tone for your gameplay. Plan your early game actions carefully.

5. Strategic Decision-making: Analyze the evolving game state, make calculated decisions, and predict opponents' moves.

6. Resource Management: Manage resources, territories, or assets efficiently to gain advantages over opponents.

7. Long-term Planning: Develop a long-term strategy, focusing on victory conditions while adapting to the ever-changing landscape.

8. Interaction: Engage with opponents diplomatically or competitively to forge alliances or seize opportunities.

9. Tactical Maneuvers: Execute tactical maneuvers that outwit opponents and maximize your chances of victory.

10. Claim Victory: Achieve victory conditions specific to the game. Revel in the satisfaction of a well-executed strategy.

Benefits:

- Cognitive Stimulation: Strategy games exercise critical thinking, problem-solving, and strategic planning skills.

- Friendly Competition: Strategic challenges create an intellectually engaging and friendly competitive environment.

Activity 4: Party Games: Unleash Creativity and Laughter

Party board games inject a dose of creativity and lightheartedness into gatherings, sparking laughter and social interaction.

Step-by-Step Instructions:

1. Pick a Game: A party game like Telestrations or The Resistance is designed for larger groups and fosters interaction.
2. Explain the Rules: Explain the game's rules, emphasizing the creative or social aspects that players will engage with.
3. Create Teams: Divide players into teams or assign roles, depending on the game. Ensure everyone understands their roles.
4. Engage Creatively: Participate in creative challenges, drawing, acting, or deciphering clues based on the game's requirements.
5. Social Interaction: Interact with teammates and opponents through playful banter, creative interpretations, and collaboration.
6. Friendly Competition: Embrace the competitive spirit while maintaining a lighthearted atmosphere. Enjoy the humorous mishaps that unfold.
7. Celebrate Efforts: Celebrate creative efforts, amusing interpretations, and the fun moments that arise during the game.

Benefits:

- Creativity: Players tap into their creative wells, expressing ideas through drawings, acting, or wordplay.
- Stress Relief: Light-hearted gameplay acts as a stress reliever and energizer, fostering a positive mood.

Activity 5: DIY Board Games: Crafted Fun and Learning

Designing your own board game unleashes creativity and provides an opportunity to learn about game design, rules, and artistic expression.

Step-by-Step Instructions:

1. Brainstorm Ideas: As a family, brainstorm game concepts, themes, and mechanics. Let the imagination flow.
2. Design the Board: Create a game board using materials like cardboard, paper, or digital tools. Incorporate spaces, paths, or regions.
3. Craft Game Components: Design and craft game pieces, cards, dice, or any elements required for gameplay.
4. Define Rules: Collaboratively establish game rules, victory conditions, and mechanics that ensure balance and engaging gameplay.
5. Test and Refine: Playtest the game to identify flaws, imbalances, or areas needing improvement. Refine rules and mechanics accordingly.
6. Artistic Expression: Encourage artistic expression through designing visuals, illustrations, and thematic elements.
7. Play Your Creation: Enjoy playing the game you've created together. Celebrate the unique aspects and creativity of your homemade game.

Benefits:s

- Creative Outlet: DIY games nurture creativity by allowing players to shape their own rules, designs, and gameplay mechanics.
- Collaboration: Designing a game together fosters collaboration, communication, and compromise among family members.

Kids board step game

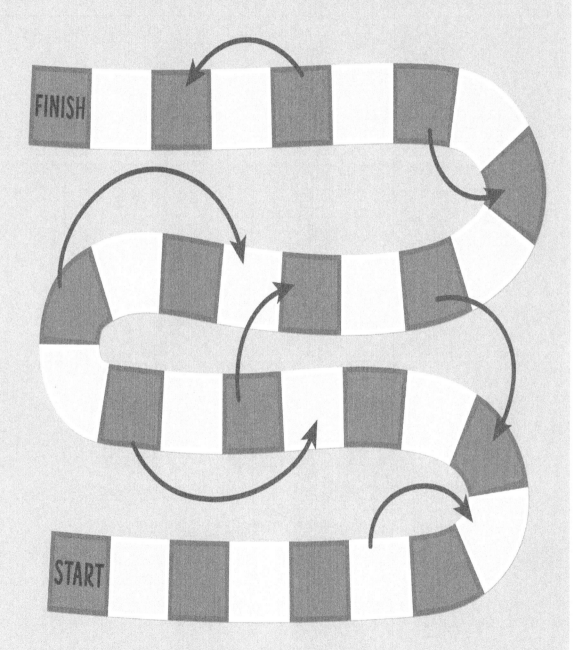

Game nights are the perfect solution for screen-free family fun. Not only do they provide an opportunity for family bonding, but they also help children develop valuable skills like critical thinking, teamwork, and problem-solving. Whether you're playing classic games, cooperative games, strategy games, party games, or creating your own DIY board game, there is always something for everyone to enjoy.

Scavenger Hunts

In a world often dominated by screens, scavenger hunts present a refreshing opportunity for families to disconnect, bond, and embark on exciting adventures together. From classic hunts to themed explorations, this section is a treasure trove of scavenger hunt ideas that kindle the spirit of teamwork and ignite creativity, all while fostering beautiful memories.

Activity 6: Classic Scavenger Hunt: Traditional Thrills Await

Classic scavenger hunts offer timeless excitement as families work together to uncover hidden treasures within a set time frame.

Step-by-Step Instructions:

1. Create the List: Craft a list of items to be found. Tailor it to your location, whether indoors or outdoors. Make it diverse and engaging.
2. Set the Rules: Establish guidelines, such as collecting one item per person or assigning specific items to individuals.
3. Gather Supplies: Provide participants with bags, baskets, or containers to collect their findings.
4. Begin the Hunt: Announce the start and let the adventure unfold as family members seek out items on the list.
5. Collaborate: Encourage teamwork by assisting each other in finding items. Share strategies and discoveries.
6. Track Progress: As items are found, check them off the list. Keep track of time to maintain excitement.
7. Finish Line: Once the time is up, gather to compare findings and celebrate the collective efforts.

Benefits:

- Family Bonding: Classic hunts encourage communication, collaboration, and shared achievement.
- Observation Skills: Participants sharpen their observation skills while searching for items.

Activity 7: Themed Scavenger Hunt: Igniting Creativity Through Themes

Themed scavenger hunts infuse creativity and enthusiasm by centering the adventure around specific interests, from nature to photography.

Step-by-Step Instructions:

1. Choose the Theme: Select a theme aligned with your family's interests, such as nature, colors, or music.

2. Craft the List: Design a list of items or tasks related to the chosen theme. Incorporate a mix of easy and challenging elements.

3. Gather Tools: Equip participants with tools that enhance the experience, such as cameras for a photography-themed hunt.

4. Commence the Hunt: Reveal the theme and task participants with finding or capturing items that fit the theme.

5. Creative Interpretation: Encourage participants to interpret the theme creatively, sparking innovation and imagination.

6. Share Discoveries: Reconvene to share findings or creations. Discuss the thought process behind each discovery.

7. Acknowledge Creativity: Celebrate not just the items found but also the inventive ways the theme was embraced.

Benefits:
- Creative Expression: Themed hunts nurture creativity and imaginative thinking.
- Memorable Moments: The hunt's theme creates unique memories tied to a shared experience.

Activity 8: Puzzle Scavenger Hunt: Unraveling Challenges Together

Puzzle scavenger hunts merge brain-teasing challenges with the thrill of discovery, offering an intellectually stimulating adventure.

Step-by-Step Instructions:
1. Craft Puzzles: Devise puzzles and riddles that lead to the location of items. Include logic puzzles, anagrams, or codes.

2. Create Clues: Develop clues that progressively unveil the next puzzle or location, forming a trail of challenges.

3. Distribute Clues: Hand out the initial clue to start the hunt. Each solved puzzle leads to the next step.

4. Solve as a Team: Collaborate to solve puzzles, pooling diverse strengths and perspectives.

5. Navigate Challenges: Overcome the puzzle hurdles to reach the final location where a prize or item awaits.

6. Celebrate Achievements: Commend everyone's puzzle-solving prowess and relish the accomplishment together.

Benefits:
- Critical Thinking: Puzzle hunts stimulate analytical thinking and problem-solving skills.
- Collaborative Spirit: Participants collaborate to decode clues, enhancing teamwork.

Activity 9: Glow-in-the-Dark Scavenger Hunt: Illuminating Nighttime Adventure

Introduction: A glow-in-the-dark scavenger hunt adds a touch of enchantment to evenings, transforming the hunt into a magical escapade.

Step-by-Step Instructions:

1. Glowing Preparations: Set the stage using glow-in-the-dark paints, stickers, or items hidden under black lights.
2. Hide Items: Conceal glow-in-the-dark items throughout the designated area, creating an intriguing landscape.
3. Equip with Black Lights: Provide participants with black lights or UV flashlights to uncover the hidden treasures.
4. Explore the Darkness: Embark on the adventure, discovering glowing surprises along the way.
5. Create Clues: Incorporate clues or challenges that lead participants to the next glowing discovery.
6. Celebrate Discoveries: Revel in the magic of glowing finds and celebrate the shared adventure.

Benefits:

- Magical Experience: Glow-in-the-dark hunts infuse an element of wonder and magic into the adventure.
- Nighttime Bonding: Engaging in an activity after dark enhances family togetherness.

Activity 10: Around the House Scavenger Hunt: Indoor Delights

When the weather or circumstances keep you indoors, an around-the-house scavenger hunt promises indoor excitement and connection.

Step-by-Step Instructions:

1. Compile a List: Assemble a list of items found within the house. Ensure a mix of easy and challenging items.
2. Distribute the List: Hand out the list to participants, sparking anticipation for the indoor adventure.
3. Search and Seek: Engage in a lively search throughout the house, seeking items listed on the scavenger hunt.
4. Show and Share: Gather the items as they are found. Share interesting or amusing aspects of each discovery.
5. Creative Connections: Use the hunt to explore your living space in novel ways, connecting with familiar surroundings.
6. Celebrate the Hunt: Celebrate not just the items found but the laughter and interaction enjoyed along the way.

Benefits:

- Indoor Adventure: Around-the-house hunts offer indoor excitement and exploration.

- Observational Skills: Participants fine-tune their observation skills while engaging in an indoor quest.

Scavenger hunts are a great way for families to bond, engage more in screen-free activities, and have fun while being creative. The options are endless, and you can customize the hunt according to your family's interests and preferences. So, plan a scavenger hunt for your family and create fantastic memories.

Storytelling and Writing Sessions

Engaging in storytelling and writing sessions as a family is a heartwarming way to cultivate connections and kindle creativity. These activities offer a canvas for shared imagination and facilitate emotional and intellectual growth in children. In this section, you'll explore the magic of storytelling and writing sessions as remarkable screen-free family endeavors.

Storytelling sessions can help parents and children unleash their creativity.
https://www.pexels.com/photo/topless-man-covering-face-with-hands-7504929/

Activity 11: Storytelling Sessions: Crafting Tales from the Heart

Storytelling sessions are portals to enchanting worlds that can be woven anytime, anywhere, without the need for equipment or technology.

Step-by-Step Instructions:

1. Choose the Moment: Set the stage for storytelling during bedtime, meals, or family gatherings.
2. Take Turns: Invite each family member to take turns sharing stories about their day, cherished experiences, or beloved memories.
3. Build Upon Novels: Elevate the experience by extending the narratives of the novels you're reading. Introduce new characters, settings, or imaginative twists.
4. Embrace Creativity: Encourage inventive storytelling by embracing unexpected twists, vibrant characters, and imaginative scenarios.

5. Active Listening: Engage in active listening as each family member shares their tale, fostering appreciation for each other's creativity.

Benefits:

- Family Bonding: Storytelling sessions create bonds as family members share, listen, and engage in each other's narratives.
- Imagination Enhancement: The open-ended nature of storytelling nurtures creativity and imaginative thinking.

Activity 12: Writing Sessions: Penning Creativity and Imagination

Writing sessions allow family members to channel their creativity and explore the limitless expanse of imagination.

Step-by-Step Instructions:

1. Designate Writing Time: Set aside a dedicated time during the week for family writing sessions.
2. Generate Prompts: Provide prompts that spark creativity or use picture books as inspiration for your child's writing journey.
3. Encourage Exploration: Urge your child to explore a spectrum of topics, from fantastical tales to real-life adventures.
4. Shared Space: Write together in a shared space, fostering a sense of togetherness while pursuing individual creativity.
5. Celebrate Diversity: Celebrate the uniqueness of each family member's writing style and ideas, promoting self-expression.

Benefits:

- Creative Outlet: Writing sessions provide a creative outlet for imaginative expression.
- Language Skills: Participants enhance their language skills, vocabulary, and writing proficiency.
- Confidence Building: Sharing written work fosters confidence and a sense of accomplishment.

Activity 13: Storytelling with Props: Enchanting Narratives Unfold

Elevate storytelling sessions with a touch of whimsy by introducing props that infuse interactive magic into the narrative.

Step-by-Step Instructions:

1. Gather Props: Collect an array of props like soft toys, hats, or random objects that can be woven into stories.
2. Prop Selection: Allow your child to select a prop; this becomes a catalyst for their storytelling adventure.
3. Interactive Storytelling: As your child narrates their tale, encourage family members to embody the characters using the chosen props.
4. Immersive Experience: Immerse in the story as it unfolds with props, breathing life into characters and scenarios.
5. Rotating Roles: Let each family member choose a prop and take turns telling enchanting stories.

Benefits:

- Immersive Engagement: Props turn storytelling into an immersive experience, sparking creativity and participation.
- Family Interaction: The interactive element deepens family engagement and sparks laughter and shared delight.

Activity 14: Collaborative Storytelling: A Tapestry of Shared Imagination

Collaborative storytelling is a dynamic avenue to foster teamwork, creativity, and effective communication among family members.

Step-by-Step Instructions:

1. Initiate the Tale: Start the storytelling journey with a captivating opening, setting the stage for collaborative creation.
2. Passing the Baton: After a segment of the story, pass the storytelling "baton" to the next family member to continue the narrative.
3. Twists and Turns: Encourage creative contributions by adding surprising twists, unexpected characters, and imaginative settings.
4. Inclusive Participation: Ensure each family member has a chance to contribute, embracing diverse perspectives.
5. Dynamic Progression: As the story unfolds, witness the evolving tale shaped by each storyteller's input.
6. Conclusion: Bring the narrative to a satisfying close, celebrating the collective journey of imagination.

Benefits:

- Shared Creativity: Family members contribute unique elements, resulting in a tapestry of creativity.
- Joy of Creation: Witnessing the evolving story fosters a sense of shared accomplishment and delight.

Activity 15: Writing Competitions: A Literary Voyage of Fun

Infuse excitement into writing sessions by transforming them into friendly competitions, kindling enthusiasm and creativity.

Step-by-Step Instructions:

1. Set Competition Intervals: Designate regular intervals for writing competitions – weekly or monthly, based on preference.
2. Choose Themes or Prompts: Assign themes or prompts that challenge participants' creativity while inspiring their written work.
3. Writing Window: Allocate a specific time frame for participants to craft their stories based on the given theme.

4. Read Aloud: Have each participant read their stories aloud, sharing their imaginative creations with the family.

5. Voting and Recognition: Engage in voting to determine the winning story. Recognize and celebrate each participant's efforts.

6. Prizes and Rewards: Award the winner with a chosen prize – a favorite snack or a day of family fun.

Benefits:

- Friendly Competition: Writing competitions infuse fun and motivation into the creative process.
- Creative Challenge: Themes and prompts challenge participants to think outside the box and explore new horizons.

Storytelling and writing sessions can be a great way to engage your children's imaginations and develop their communication and creativity skills. These activities also help families spend quality time together and foster a love for storytelling and reading or even awaken a new talent. Furthermore, the lack of screens during these activities should lead to a more enjoyable and memorable experience for the whole family. So, set aside some time every week to explore your imagination through storytelling and writing sessions.

DIY Science Experiments

In an age dominated by screens, fostering creativity and exploration beyond technology becomes essential. One remarkable way to achieve this is by conducting captivating science experiments at home. These hands-on activities engage, educate, and bring families closer together. Here, we delve into captivating DIY science experiments that promise screen-free family excitement.

Activity 16: Make a Lava Lamp: Unveil the Magic of Chemistry

Crafting a lava lamp is a mesmerizing science experiment that promises wonder and amazement.

Step-by-Step Instructions:

1. Gather Materials: Collect a jar, water, oil, food coloring, and Alka-Seltzer tablets.

2. Water and Color: Fill a quarter of the jar with water and add a few drops of food coloring for a vibrant effect.

3. Oil and Jar Filling: Pour oil into the jar until it's three-quarters full, creating distinct layers.

4. Alka-Seltzer Magic: Break an Alka-Seltzer tablet into small pieces and drop them into the jar.

5. Observing the Transformation: Witness the captivating display as the tablet reacts with water, causing oil bubbles to rise, resembling a lava lamp.

Benefits:

- Scientific Phenomenon: Unveil the chemistry behind the mesmerizing motion.
- Visual Delight: Engage in captivating visual observation as the experiment unfolds.

Lava Lamp Mini Shaker

Activity 17: DIY Slime: A Sensory Exploration

Crafting your slime offers a tactile and imaginative journey into the world of science.

Step-by-Step Instructions:

1. Gather Ingredients: Collect PVA glue, borax powder or saline solution, and optional food coloring.
2. Mixing and Kneading: Combine the glue with Borax or saline solution until the mixture forms a cohesive ball.
3. Adding Color: Enhance the visual appeal by introducing food coloring and kneading until the color is evenly distributed.
4. Texture Exploration: Experience the tactile joy of stretching and manipulating the slime.

Benefits:

- Tactile Engagement: Creating and playing with slime provides a sensory-rich experience.
- Exploration of Properties: Participants explore the behavior of non-Newtonian fluids.

Activity 18: Create a Simple Circuit: Illuminating Electricity Basics

Introducing your children to the world of simple circuits lays the foundation for understanding electrical concepts.

Step-by-Step Instructions:

1. Assemble Materials: Prepare a battery, wire, and a lightbulb.
2. Wiring the Circuit: Connect the battery and lightbulb using the wire, forming a closed circuit.
3. Switch On: Activate the circuit by turning on the switch and observing the illumination of the lightbulb.

Benefits:

- Introduction to Electricity: Basic circuits offer a hands-on understanding of electrical flow.
- Visual Learning: Witnessing the lightbulb illuminate enhances comprehension.

Activity 19: Make a Crystal Snowflake: Winter Wonder in Science

Crafting crystal snowflakes blends winter wonder with science exploration.

Step-by-Step Instructions:

1. Gather Supplies: Collect Borax, pipe cleaners, boiling water, and a jar.
2. Pipe Cleaner Shapes: Bend pipe cleaners into snowflake designs, embracing creativity.
3. Borax Solution: Dissolve Borax in boiling water, creating a supersaturated solution.
4. Suspending Snowflakes: Suspend pipe cleaner snowflakes in the solution overnight.
5. Crystal Formation: Wake up to exquisite crystal-covered snowflakes in the morning.

Benefits:

- Crystal Growth Understanding: Witness the process of crystal formation firsthand.
- Art and Science Blend: Crafting snowflake shapes adds an artistic flair to the experiment.

Activity 20: Balloon Rocket Experiment: Propelling Physics Fun

The balloon rocket experiment introduces physics in a playful and captivating manner.

Step-by-Step Instructions:

1. Arrange the Setup: Prepare a long string, a straw, a balloon, and tape.
2. String Anchoring: Thread the string through the straw, securing it to two fixed objects across the room.
3. Balloon Attachment: Inflate the balloon and tape it to the straw.
4. Air-Powered Zoom: Release the balloon, allowing it to propel along the string due to escaping air.

Benefits:

- Physics Exploration: Experience Newton's third law of motion in action.
- Interactive Learning: Witness the experiment's outcome firsthand, promoting engagement.

The goal isn't to demonize technology entirely but to create pockets of real-world connection within your digital life. By swapping screens for DIY board games, hands-on science experiments, and collaborative storytelling sessions, you've opened doors to laughter, shared experiences, and deeper bonds. These screen-free activities are investments in family memories. They'll foster creativity, communication, and problem-solving skills that will resonate long after the games are stored and stories are finished.

Chapter 3: Outdoor Adventure Ideas

From hiking along scenic trails to camping under the stars, the great outdoors offers endless opportunities for fun and exploration. Get your heart pumping with a whitewater rafting trip, or test your skills on a thrilling zip line course. No matter what your family enjoys, outdoor adventure is the perfect way to disconnect from screens and connect meaningfully to nature and each other. So, gear up and prepare to embark on an unforgettable journey that will create memories to last a lifetime!

Inspired by the YouTube channel Fernweh Chronicles, this chapter invites you to embark on outdoor activities with your family. Nature is the perfect playground for families, allowing parents and children to create special memories and deepen relationships. Whether you're a fan of the outdoors or just starting, the 15 activities listed in this chapter will bring your family closer together while enjoying the wonders of nature.

Activity 21: Nature Walks

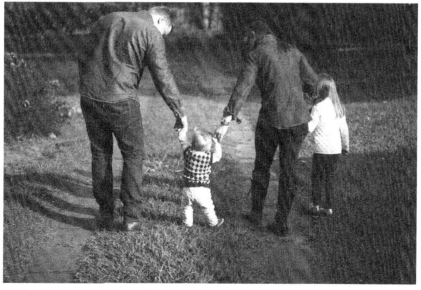

Taking a nature walk as a family will allow you to soak up the beauty of the natural world.
https://www.pexels.com/photo/family-walking-on-path-1682497/

Nature walks offer a fantastic opportunity for families to spend quality time together while soaking up all the beauty and goodness the natural world has to offer. One can never underestimate the benefits of fresh air, exercise, and sunshine on our physical and emotional well-being. These are precisely what families get when they hit the trails for a nature walk. Whether a short stroll around the neighborhood park or a longer hike up a mountain trail, there's always something to discover and appreciate in nature.

Step-by-Step Instructions:

1. Choose a Trail: Select a trail suited to your family's fitness level and interests. Opt for shorter paths for younger participants.
2. Dress Comfortably: Wear weather-appropriate attire and comfortable footwear to fully relish the experience.
3. Pack Essentials: Bring essentials like water, sunscreen, insect repellent, and a small first-aid kit.
4. Capture the Moment: Equip yourselves with a camera or smartphone to capture the beauty of nature.
5. Embrace Discovery: Encourage family members to explore, ask questions, and appreciate the natural surroundings.
6. Engage the Senses: Listen to bird songs, breathe in the fresh air, and feel the textures of leaves and rocks.
7. Mindful Moments: Pause along the way for mindfulness, allowing each family member to soak in the tranquility.

Benefits:

- Stress Relief: The serene environment aids in stress reduction and emotional well-being.
- Natural Learning: Nature is a dynamic classroom, fostering curiosity and learning.

As parents plan their excursions, the environment should always be on their minds. It's essential to respect and care for nature as we enjoy it so we can continue to experience its wonders for years to come. With preparation, safety in mind, and flexibility in plans, nature walks are a surefire way to create unforgettable memories as a family.

Activity 22: Geocaching

This thrilling adventure is a modern-day treasure hunt that has become a global phenomenon for good reason. Geocaching is a treasure hunt with a high-tech twist. Using GPS coordinates and clues, you can uncover hidden caches all around the globe. It's a great way to discover new places, get outdoors, and challenge yourself. Plus, it's perfect for all ages, from families with children to solo adventurers.

Step-by-Step Instructions:

Gather the Essentials: Equip yourselves with a GPS device or smartphone with a geocaching app, a notepad, a pen, and small trinkets for trading.

1. Select a Cache: Browse geocaching websites or apps to choose a cache – a hidden container waiting to be discovered.
2. Navigate to Coordinates: Input cache coordinates into your GPS device or app, guiding you to the hidden treasure.

3. Search and Discover: Follow the GPS guidance to reach the cache's vicinity. Utilize hints and descriptions to narrow your search.

4. Retrieve and Trade: Once found, open the cache, sign the logbook, and explore the contents. You can trade trinkets while respecting the cache's guidelines.

5. Log Your Find: Record your discovery on the geocaching app or website to share your experience with the geocaching community.

Benefits:

- Problem-Solving: The hunt challenges problem-solving skills as you decipher clues and navigate the terrain.

- Global Community: Engage with a diverse community of geocachers, forging connections beyond borders.

Geocaching offers the perfect opportunity to teach kids about the environment and encourage them to be mindful of the natural world. So, grab your GPS device, lace up your hiking boots, and hit the trails for a geocaching adventure your family will never forget.

Activity 23: Gardening Projects

Gardening can be a wholesome and fulfilling adventure for the whole family. It brings you closer to nature and provides an opportunity for exercise and fresh air. Imagine your family outside, tending your garden, watching it flourish and grow. The opportunities are endless, from planting a vegetable garden to creating a butterfly garden. You could even take it a step further: If you have the available space, build a mini-farm with chickens or other animals.

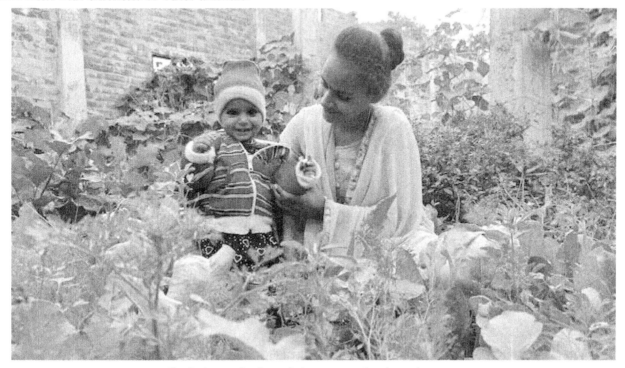

Gardening as a family can help you appreciate the environment.

Step-by-Step Instructions:

1. Select a Garden Theme: Decide on the type of garden you want.

2. Plan the Layout: Design the garden layout with input from every family member. Allocate spaces for each chosen plant.

3. Prep the Soil: Clear the chosen area of debris and enrich the soil with compost, setting the stage for healthy plant growth.

4. Planting Day: Gather the family and plant seeds or young plants according to your plan. Involve children in planting and watering.

5. Care and Nourish: Assign garden care responsibilities, from watering to weeding. Teach your children the importance of regular care.

6. Celebrate Growth: As plants flourish, celebrate their growth milestones together. Discuss the significance of each plant in the ecosystem.

7. Personalized Spaces: Allow each family member a dedicated area for personal expression, encouraging creativity through plant choice and decorations.

Benefits:

- Nurturing Bonds: Gardening fosters teamwork and a sense of shared accomplishment within the family.
- Life Skills: Gardening imparts patience, responsibility, and the joy of reaping what you sow.

Gardening is a sustainable and earth-friendly activity that makes you appreciate the environment meaningfully. With proper preparation, safety measures, and adaptability, you can ensure a fun and very visible experience for everyone.

Activity 24: RV Through National Parks

If you're looking for an adventure completely immersing you in nature, look no further than an RV trip through national parks. The idea of hitting the open road with your family in tow and exploring the stunning landscapes surrounding us is enticing, to say the least. The fresh air, the beauty of the surroundings, and the sense of freedom an RV trip provides can be a powerful experience.

Step-by-Step Instructions:

1. Plan Your Route: Research and select national parks that align with your family's interests and preferences. Design an itinerary that encompasses the best of each park.

2. Choose an RV: Opt for an RV that suits your family's size and needs. Ensure it's well-equipped for a comfortable journey. (RVs can be rented if you can't afford to buy one.)

3. Pack Essentials: Pack essentials, such as clothing, camping gear, food, water, and a first-aid kit.

4. Hit the Road: Embark on your adventure, driving through breathtaking landscapes and stopping at designated national parks.

5. Explore Nature: Enjoy outdoor activities like hiking, wildlife spotting, and scenic viewpoints. Encourage children to learn about the ecosystems.

6. Camp Under the Stars: Camp in designated areas within the parks or in nearby campgrounds. Set up a campfire, share stories, and gaze at the stars.

7. Respect Nature: Abide by park rules and Leave No Trace principles. Teach your children the importance of preserving the natural environment.

Benefits:

- Connection to Nature: RV trips foster a profound connection to nature, enriching family bonds.
- Physical Wellness: Outdoor activities promote physical fitness and well-being.

From Yosemite to Glacier National Park and everywhere in between, an endless array of national parks is waiting to be explored. With proper planning, safety measures, and flexibility, you can venture on a journey your family will never forget.

Activity 25: Go Trekking

Trekking is an adventurous way to explore new places and a fantastic opportunity to bond with your family, breathe in the fresh air, and take in stunning scenery. There's nothing quite like conquering a challenging trail together, high-fiving at the top of a mountain, and taking in a breathtaking view as a reward.

Step-by-Step Instructions:

1. Select Your Trail: Research and choose a trail suitable for your family's fitness level and interests.
2. Dress the Part: Wear comfortable, moisture-wicking clothing and sturdy footwear that offers proper support.
3. Pack Thoughtfully: Load up with essential items, such as snacks, water, a basic first-aid kit, a map, and a compass.
4. Safety First: Research the chosen trail in advance. Inform a trusted friend or family member about your plans.
5. Start the Journey: Set out on your trek with a positive attitude and a spirit of adventure. Take regular breaks to rest and enjoy the scenery.
6. Capture Memories: Bring a camera or smartphone to capture the picturesque moments along the way.
7. Bond and Connect: Engage in conversations, share stories, and play games during breaks to strengthen family bonds and create lasting memories.

Benefits:

- Physical Challenge: Trekking offers a full-body workout, boosting cardiovascular health and stamina.
- Family Bonding: Shared experiences in nature deepen connections and foster meaningful conversations.

It's essential to prepare for your trekking adventure properly. Dress appropriately, pack plenty of snacks and water, and research the trail ahead of time for information on the difficulty level and any safety concerns. And most importantly, remember to be flexible and adapt to unexpected changes in the weather or terrain.

Activity 26: Pan for Gold

Imagine a family adventure that blends the thrill of outdoor exploration with the allure of striking it rich. Panning for gold is an engaging escapade that involves teamwork, physical effort, and the excitement of discovering hidden treasures. As you plunge your hands into the earth, sift through gravel, and witness the glint of gold, you'll create enduring memories and forge unbreakable bonds with your loved ones.

Step-by-Step Instructions:

1. Select Your Location: Research local areas where gold panning is allowed. Look for spots with historical significance or areas known for gold deposits.
2. Gather Supplies: Acquire basic gold panning equipment, including a pan, shovel, and a container for collecting your findings.
3. Find the Right Spot: Head to the riverbank or a stream known for gold potential. Look for areas with slower-moving water and gravel bars.
4. Dig and Fill: Using your shovel, gather gravel and soil from the riverbed. Fill your pan about half-full with this mixture.
5. Submerge and Swirl: Submerge the pan in water, allowing water to flow in and wash away the lighter materials.
6. Fanning Technique: Use the fanning technique to remove excess material, leaving behind heavier particles that could be gold.
7. Focus on the Bottom: Tilt the pan slightly forward and gently shake it side to side to encourage gold to settle at the bottom.
8. Inspect and Collect: Carefully inspect the bottom of the pan. If you spot glimmers of gold, use tweezers or a small vial to collect your findings.

Benefits:

- Physical Activity: The process of digging, washing, and sifting engages muscles and provides a fun form of exercise.
- Bonding and Memories: As you work together to uncover gold, you create shared memories and strengthen family bonds.

With each sift of the pan, you're not just searching for gold. You're sifting through time, unearthing stories of the past, and sharing the spirit of adventure that has captivated explorers for generations. So, grab your pan, head to the riverside, and embark on a journey that promises both glittering treasures and cherished connections.

Activity 27: Clean Up, Connect, and Give Back: Family Fun with a Purpose in the Outdoors

Sunshine, fresh air, and a chance to make a difference. What better ingredients could you ask for in a family outing? Ditch the screens and head outdoors for a rewarding experience that combines community spirit with the joy of spending time in nature. Volunteering for a local park clean-up, beach clean-up, or community garden is a fantastic way to instill environmental awareness in your children while fostering teamwork and a sense of accomplishment.

Step-by-Step Instructions:

1. **Pick Your Project:** Dive into the heart of nature with a beach clean-up, or spruce up your neighborhood park. Community gardens often welcome helping hands too. Research local organizations or check online calendars for upcoming events.

2. **Gather Your Heroes:** Assemble your family heroes. From enthusiastic toddlers to responsible teens, everyone can contribute. Explain the importance of environmental stewardship and get them excited about their roles.

3. **Gear Up for Action:** Dress comfortably and weather-appropriately. Sunscreen, hats, water bottles, and snacks are essential. Don't forget reusable gloves and sturdy bags for collecting trash.

4. **Bond as You Pick:** Divide tasks according to age and abilities. Little ones can collect small litter, while older kids can tackle larger items. Teamwork makes the clean dream work.

5. **Treasure Hunt Time:** Turn trash collecting into a game. Challenge yourselves to find the most unusual piece of litter or create categories for different finds. Make it fun and educational.

6. **Celebrate Your Impact:** After a job well done, take a moment to appreciate your contribution. Discuss the positive impact you've made on the environment and your community.

Benefits:

- **Bonding Time:** Working together on a shared goal strengthens family ties and creates lasting memories.

- **Nature Connection:** Immerse yourselves in the outdoors, appreciate fresh air and sunshine, and learn about the local environment.

- **Civic Responsibility:** Instill a sense of community spirit and empower your children to make a positive difference.

- **Fitness Fun:** Get some exercise while having fun! Bending, walking, and carrying bags contribute to an active and healthy family outing.

Trade in your usual routine for an adventure with purpose. Grab your family, head outdoors, and volunteer your time for a clean-up project. You'll be amazed at the sense of accomplishment, the connection to nature, and the joy of giving back to your community, all while creating unforgettable family memories. Every little bit counts, and together, you will make a big difference.

Activity 28: Seaplane Adventure

If you're looking for an exciting way to bond with your children, a seaplane adventure is what you need. Not only will you get to ride on a unique aircraft, but you'll also be treated to breathtaking views of the ocean and surrounding landscapes. This experience will be fun and has its own educational and developmental benefits.

Step-by-Step Instructions:

1. **Choose a Reputable Provider:** Research and select a reputable seaplane tour provider that adheres to safety protocols and offers captivating routes.

2. **Plan Ahead:** Reserve your adventure in advance, ensuring availability and smooth logistics for your family.

3. **Safety Briefing:** Before takeoff, listen carefully to the safety briefing provided by the pilot. Familiarize yourselves with emergency procedures.

4. Buckle Up: Once onboard, ensure everyone is securely buckled up, ready to embark on this thrilling journey.

5. Capture the Moments: Bring along a camera or smartphone to capture the mesmerizing aerial views and the excitement on your family's faces.

6. Curiosity Unleashed: Encourage your children to ask questions about the landscape below, the plane's mechanics, and everything that piques their curiosity.

7. Enjoy the Experience: As you ascend above the water, let the sense of awe wash over you. Take in the panoramic views and cherish this moment of shared wonder.

Benefits:

- Educational Exploration: A seaplane adventure fuels children's curiosity and encourages them to learn about aviation, geography, and the natural world.

- Confidence and Adventure: Experiencing flight fosters confidence and an adventurous spirit as children engage with the world from a new perspective.

With this thrilling activity, you'll soar high above the water, taking in breathtaking views and experiencing a head rush like no other. But the benefits of a seaplane excursion go far beyond just the physical thrill. It's also a chance to connect with your loved ones, bond over a shared sense of adventure, and create memories that will last a lifetime.

Activity 29: Row Boating

Close your eyes and imagine yourself gliding through calm waters, surrounded by the beauty of nature. The gentle sounds of birds and water create a soothing symphony as you embark on a row boating adventure with your children.

Step-by-Step Instructions:

1. Choose Your Location: Research and select a suitable water body for row boating—be it a serene lake, a meandering river, or a calm inlet.

2. Safety First: Prioritize safety by equipping everyone with life jackets and ensuring you're familiar with the water's conditions.

3. Basic Rowing Technique: Familiarize your family with the basics of rowing, including how to hold the oars and navigate the boat.

4. Share Responsibilities: Assign roles to each family member, whether it's rowing, steering, or simply enjoying the ride.

5. Capture the Experience: Bring a waterproof camera or smartphone to capture the picturesque moments and the smiles on your family's faces.

6. Engage with Nature: Take moments to pause and immerse yourselves in the natural world around you.

7. Mindful Connection: Use the gentle rhythm of rowing to engage in meaningful conversations and enjoy each other's presence.

Benefits:

- Physical Activity: Row boating provides a full-body workout, enhancing cardiovascular health and building physical strength.

- Teamwork and Communication: Coordinating rowing actions fosters teamwork and communication, strengthening familial bonds.

As your family embarks on a row boating adventure, you'll bask in the beauty of nature and build cherished memories that will last a lifetime. So, gather your crew, launch your boat, and navigate the waters of togetherness and exploration.

Activity 30: Wildlife Safari

Imagine getting into a sturdy jeep and embarking on a thrilling adventure through the great outdoors with your loved ones, surrounded by the sounds and sights of majestic creatures in their natural habitat. The excitement of spotting a lion basking in the sun or a herd of grazing elephants is matched only by the emotional and physical benefits of this incredible experience.

Step-by-Step Instructions:

1. Choose Your Safari: Research and select a reputable wildlife reserve or national park known for its rich biodiversity and responsible conservation practices.
2. Guided or Self-Drive: Decide whether to embark on a guided safari with a knowledgeable ranger or opt for a self-drive adventure.
3. Pack Essentials: Prepare by packing essentials, such as binoculars, cameras, hats, sunscreen, insect repellent, and water to stay comfortable and capture memories.
4. Respect Wildlife: Emphasize the importance of respecting the animals and their habitat. Keep a safe distance and avoid disturbing their natural behaviors.
5. Stay Patient: Patience is key in wildlife observation. Spend time quietly observing and waiting for the animals to appear naturally.
6. Learn and Appreciate: Encourage your family to ask questions, learn about the animals, and appreciate the intricate balance of nature.

Benefits:

- Educational Experience: Wildlife safaris offer a unique educational opportunity for your children to learn about different species and ecosystems.
- Nature Immersion: Immerse yourselves in the natural world, gaining a deeper understanding of the delicate balance of life in the wild.

A wildlife safari is an exhilarating escapade and a rare opportunity to recharge and reconnect with nature, giving you a much-needed break from the hustle and bustle of daily life.

Activity 31: Stargazing

Gazing up at the stars has been a source of inspiration and discovery since time immemorial. This activity is more than just a fun experience. It encourages your little ones to explore their curiosity and creativity. Through stargazing, children learn about our universe's vastness and the planets and understand astronomy better.

Materials Needed:

- Telescope or Binoculars: Enhance your stargazing with a telescope or binoculars to observe celestial bodies more closely.

- Star Maps or Apps: Use star maps or smartphone apps to identify constellations and planets visible in the night sky.
- Blankets and Pillows: Create a cozy space for your family to lie down and comfortably gaze at the stars.
- Warm Clothing: Dress warmly to ensure comfort during nighttime stargazing sessions.
- Flashlights: Red-filtered flashlights are ideal for preserving your night vision.

Step-by-Step Instructions:

1. Choose a Clear Night: Pick a night with minimal light pollution for optimal stargazing visibility.
2. Location Matters: Find a quiet, open area away from city lights, such as your backyard, a park, or a camping site.
3. Set Up Comfortably: Lay out blankets and pillows to make a comfortable space for everyone to lie down and gaze at the sky.
4. Learn the Basics: Before heading out, familiarize yourself with a few key constellations and planets visible that night.
5. Use Star Maps or Apps: Use star maps or stargazing apps to help identify celestial bodies and constellations as you spot them.
6. Engage Curiosity: Encourage questions and discussions about what you're seeing. Explore topics like planets, stars, galaxies, and the cosmos.

Benefits for Families:

- Quality Time: Stargazing brings families together in a serene setting, fostering bonding and meaningful conversations.
- Wonder and Awe: Observing the vastness of the universe evokes a sense of wonder and humility, igniting curiosity in children.

By taking your little ones out to look up at the night sky, you introduce them to a beautiful world beyond our planet and create precious memories with your kids. Stargazing is a fantastic experience and an excellent way to bond with your family.

Activity 32: Camping

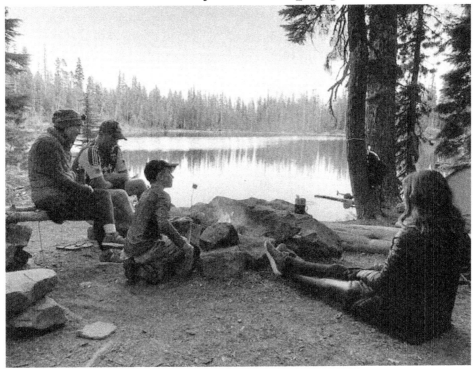

Camping can encourage your children to explore.

https://unsplash.com/photos/8-jqqr-rpo0?utm_source=unsplash&utm_medium=referral&utm_content=creditShareLink

When was the last time you spent time with your family, away from the hustle and bustle of modern life? Exploring the outdoors is a beautiful way to connect and experience nature's beauty together. Put up a tent, gather around a campfire, and sing songs while roasting marshmallows. Camping is the perfect getaway for you and your children.

Materials Needed:

- Tents and Sleeping Bags: Ensure you have suitable tents and cozy sleeping bags for everyone.
- Campfire Supplies: Pack firewood, matches, and fire starters for safe and enjoyable campfires.
- Cooking Gear: Don't forget a portable stove, pots, pans, utensils, and other cooking essentials.
- Food and Snacks: Plan and pack meals, snacks, and ingredients for a variety of dishes.
- Water and Hydration: Carry ample water bottles and a water purification system if needed.
- Clothing and Footwear: Pack weather-appropriate clothing, including rain gear and comfortable footwear.
- Outdoor Equipment: Consider bringing hiking gear, binoculars, and nature identification guides.
- First-Aid Kit: Ensure you have a well-stocked first-aid kit for any emergencies.

Step-by-Step Instructions:

1. Choose a Camping Site: Research and choose a camping site that suits your family's preferences and level of outdoor experience.

2. Prepare Camping Gear: Gather and check all camping gear, ensuring everything is in good condition and properly functioning.

3. Pack Essential Supplies: Pack tents, sleeping bags, clothing, food, cooking equipment, and other essentials.

4. Set Up Camp: Upon arrival, set up your tents, arrange sleeping areas, and establish a comfortable campsite layout.

5. Campfire Creation: Build a safe and controlled campfire in designated fire rings or areas.

6. Cook Delicious Meals: Utilize your cooking gear to prepare meals, allowing your family to enjoy hearty and nutritious food.

7. Bond around the Campfire: As the sun sets, gather around the campfire for storytelling, singing, and roasting marshmallows.

8. Practice Leave No Trace: Respect the environment by leaving your campsite clean and minimizing your impact on nature.

Benefits:

- Skill Development: Camping encourages problem-solving, critical thinking, teamwork, and adaptability.

- Technology Detox: Camping allows for a break from screens and technology, enabling true face-to-face interactions.

Camping is a great way to spend quality time with your family. It allows you to bond and create lasting memories in the great outdoors. So put on your backpacks, pack your tents and some snacks, and start planning for an unforgettable camping adventure!

Activity 33: Air Balloon Ride

Imagine the excitement of taking to the skies with your family in an air balloon! The breathtaking views, the serenity and peace up in the clouds, and the feeling of floating on a breeze are truly magical experiences.

Step-by-Step Instructions:

1. Choose a Reputable Operator: Research and select a reputable air balloon ride operator known for safety and exceptional experiences.

2. Plan Ahead: Make reservations in advance and choose a time that suits your family's schedule and preferences.

3. Dress Comfortably: Wear weather-appropriate clothing and comfortable shoes for the journey.

4. Arrival and Preparation: Arrive at the designated location and listen attentively to the pilot's safety instructions.

5. Take Off: As the balloon inflates, experience the thrill of takeoff, feeling the gentle lift as the balloon ascends.

6. Breathtaking Views: As you rise above the landscape, marvel at the breathtaking panoramic views below.

Benefits:

- Memorable Experience: An air balloon ride creates lasting memories that you and your family will cherish for years to come.

- Unique Perspective: Seeing the world from above provides a unique and captivating perspective on familiar landscapes.

The experience of floating in an air balloon will provide your family with some beautiful memories, help children appreciate nature's beauty from a different perspective, and awaken their sense of adventure.

Activity 34: Snow Skiing

A fantastic skiing adventure can be just the thing to get the family together and enjoy a thrilling experience with each other. Snow skiing is a sport that encourages your children to stay physically active while having fun. It can also help them learn the importance of patience, practice, and safety. In addition to the physical benefits, skiing will help your kids learn about teamwork.

Materials Needed:

- Ski equipment (skis, poles, boots, helmets)

- Ski clothing (waterproof jacket, pants, gloves)

- Goggles to protect eyes from sun and snow glare

Step-by-Step Instructions:

1. Choose the Right Destination: Research and select a skiing destination suitable for your family's skiing abilities, whether beginner or experienced.

2. Rent or Buy Equipment: If you don't already have skiing gear, rent or buy skis, poles, boots, and helmets for each family member.

3. Dress for Success: Wear appropriate ski clothing to keep warm and dry on the slopes, including waterproof jackets, pants, gloves, and goggles.

4. Safety First: Attend a brief lesson on skiing basics, including how to put on and use your gear, skiing techniques, and safety measures.

5. Start on Gentle Slopes: Begin on beginner slopes to build confidence and get comfortable with the skiing motion.

6. Take Skiing Lessons: Enroll in skiing lessons for beginners or intermediate skiers to improve your skills and gain confidence.

Benefits:

- Physical Activity: Skiing is a fantastic way to stay active and engage in a full-body workout while having fun.

- Life Skills: Learning to ski teaches patience, perseverance, and the importance of practice in achieving goals.

With ski resorts, snow parks, and other activities like zip lining and sledding, you and your family can enjoy a great time together, learning something new while having fun. So, grab your ski gear and hit the slopes for an unforgettable skiing experience!

Activity 35: Barbecue

Picture a sun-kissed afternoon in your backyard, with the tantalizing aroma of grilled food wafting through the air and the joyous sounds of laughter as your family gathers for a delightful barbecue. This culinary adventure isn't just about indulging in delicious food. It's a chance to create lasting memories while sharing the joy of cooking and quality time with your loved ones.

Materials Needed:

- Grill (charcoal, gas, or electric)
- Grilling utensils (tongs, brushes)
- Ingredients for chosen dishes
- Seasonings and marinades
- Outdoor seating and decorations

Step-by-Step Instructions:

1. Plan the Menu: Decide on a menu that includes a variety of foods to grill, such as burgers, hot dogs, vegetables, and even skewers.
2. Preparation Time: Gather the necessary ingredients, seasonings, and marinades for your chosen dishes. Invite your kids to help with preparations.
3. Fire Up the Grill: Preheat the grill and ensure it's clean and ready for cooking. Make sure you have the appropriate tools, such as tongs and brushes.
4. Grill the Goodness: Carefully place your chosen items on the grill and cook them to perfection.
5. Involvement of Children: Encourage your children to help with the grilling process. Teach them about grill safety and the art of flipping burgers.
6. Set the Scene: Arrange a comfortable outdoor dining area with seating, decorations, and a cozy atmosphere for the family to enjoy.

Benefits:

- Culinary Skills: Involving your children in the preparation and cooking process fosters valuable culinary skills and a sense of accomplishment.
- Life Lessons: Cooking teaches patience, cooperation, and the value of teamwork while preparing a meal together.

Gathering around the grill isn't just about savoring scrumptious food. It's an opportunity for your family to connect, engage in meaningful conversations, and enjoy each other's company in a relaxed and enjoyable atmosphere. As you share laughs, stories, and bites of mouthwatering food, your family barbecue will become a cherished tradition that brings everyone closer together. So, light up the grill, let the flavors dance, and celebrate the joy of cooking and togetherness in your backyard haven.

Whether you're in the mood for a scenic hike, a thrilling rafting trip, or a relaxing day at the beach, there's no shortage of possibilities when it comes to outdoor fun. This chapter provides some beautiful ideas on how to spend quality time with your family and create lasting memories together. From geocaching, nature walks, camping, air balloon rides, skiing, and barbecues, these adventures offer the perfect opportunity for bonding and creating lasting memories with your loved ones. So, it's time to grab the family and start exploring!

Chapter 4: Creative Souls: Unleash Your Inner Artists

There's an artist inside all of us waiting to be unleashed, and what better way to bring it out than with family? Creative souls can find inspiration in the most unexpected places, and sharing the process with loved ones makes it all the more rewarding. Whether painting, writing, pottery, or any other art form, making art together can deepen connections and build lasting memories. So, gather your family, grab some supplies, and let your inner artists run wild.

Activity 36: Creative Collages

Collages can be personalized to suit your family's style and interests.

From beginners to experienced artists, collages are the perfect creative outlet for anyone. Spend quality time with the family as you cut, paste, and create beautiful art together. Be it photographs or magazine clippings, the possibilities for collage materials are endless. In addition, collages can be personalized to represent your family's unique style and interests. With this activity, you'll tap into your creativity, bond with your loved ones, and create beautiful memories. Here's all you need to get started:

Materials Needed

- Scissors
- Glue or tape
- A variety of magazines, newspapers, cardboard, and other materials
- A board or canvas for the collage

Step-by-Step Instructions

1. Gather your supplies and decide on a theme for your collage.
2. Arrange the materials in an aesthetically pleasing pattern.
3. Cut and glue the pieces to your board or canvas.
4. Let your artwork dry before displaying it proudly!

Additional Ideas

- Create a family tree collage with pictures of your relatives
- Cut up old magazines and newspaper articles to create an abstract work of art
- Have each family member make their own unique collage. This can be a great display piece when hung side by side!
- Explore the world of mixed media and incorporate 3D elements like buttons, fabric, found objects, etc., into your collage.

Remember to have fun and enjoy the creative process regardless of your project type. Then, celebrate your masterpiece with a family photo or an online post. Sharing your artwork is a great way to show off the beautiful bond you have created together.

Activity 37: Family Murals

Creating art together as a family is a great way to foster a more profound sense of connection and creativity within your household. With family murals in particular, you can unleash your inner artist and collaborate to create something extraordinary. Whether creating a work of art to adorn the walls of your home or simply using it as an opportunity to bond, family murals are a fun and rewarding experience that everyone can enjoy. Don't worry if you're not the most artistically inclined person. The beauty of working on a mural is that everyone can contribute.

Materials Needed

- A large canvas or wall
- Acrylic paint in various colors
- Paintbrushes of different sizes
- Other materials (fabric, paper, beads), if desired
- Protective sheeting to cover the floor or wall

Step-by-Step Instructions

1. Start by cleaning the wall or canvas and laying down protective sheeting to cover the floor or wall.
2. Have each family member devise a design for their mural section and sketch it out.
3. Begin painting the mural one section at a time.
4. Once all the sections are complete, admire your masterpiece!

Additional Ideas

- Include meaningful symbols, quotes, or images that represent the family
- Make each mural section unique by including fabric, paper, beads, and more
- Have each family member sign their section with a message of love or encouragement
- Remember to document your creative process with photos or videos!

Working together on a family mural is an enriching way to express yourselves as individuals while uniting as a unit. The perfect combination of art and connection will leave a lasting impression on everyone. So, grab a paintbrush and let the creative juices flow.

Activity 38: Group Weaving Projects

Group weaving projects are an opportunity to get together with your loved ones and make something beautiful. Whether you are a seasoned weaver or a beginner, there are endless possibilities to explore. This section will provide all the information you need to create a wonderful weaving project with your loved ones.

Materials Needed

- Weaving loom or frame
- Yarn, thread, or wool
- Recycled materials or fabric scraps
- Scissors
- Tapestry needle
- Comb or fork
- Optional embellishments like beads, buttons, and feathers.

Step-by-Step Instructions

1. Set up your loom or frame by following the instructions on your purchased loom or by researching a tutorial on how to make your own.
2. Tie a ribbon, piece of yarn, or string to the top of the loom or frame to create a starting point.
3. Begin your weaving project by wrapping the yarn or wool around the loom or frame in a horizontal direction. Make sure to pull the thread tightly to avoid gaps.
4. After the first row is complete, push the yarn down with a fork or a comb to keep the row compact.
5. Start the second row by taking a piece of yarn or wool and weaving it under and over the first row of threads. Repeat this process and continue pushing down the rows as needed.
6. To change colors or add texture, tie or weave the next color into the end of the yarn or wool and continue weaving.

7. Once you have reached the desired length, tie off the end of the yarn and cut any excess.

8. Carefully remove the weaving project from your loom or frame, then tie the loose ends together or sew a border piece around the project.

Additional Ideas

- Consider making a collaborative weaving project where everyone contributes by adding their weaves.

- Make a themed weaving, such as a holiday decoration or a piece of art for a specific room in your home.

- Use different materials like ribbon, tulle, or lace to add texture and dimension to your weaving project.

Regardless of your skill level, you can enjoy the process of weaving and exploring different textures and colors. So, grab your loom or frame and various materials, and enjoy some quality time with your family or friends while unleashing your inner artist.

Activity 39: Family Talent Show

Call all aspiring singers, dancers, comedians, and magicians. Dust off your imaginary mics, grab your DIY props and get ready to dazzle the world (or at least your immediate family) with the ultimate family talent show. This activity is the perfect recipe for a night of laughter, memories, and unleashing hidden talents you never knew existed. What are you waiting for? It's time to turn your living room into a miniature Vegas stage.

Step-by-Step Instructions:

1. **Spread the Word:** Announce the upcoming extravaganza. Get everyone excited about showcasing their hidden (or not-so-hidden) talents. Let imaginations run wild with ideas for songs, dances, skits, magic tricks, or even puppet shows.

2. **Brainstorm:** Gather the family and have a brainstorming session. Encourage participation from even the shyest members. There's a talent for everyone. Make it a collaborative effort, allowing everyone to contribute ideas and costumes.

3. **Practice Makes Perfect (Optional):** While spontaneity is always welcome, a little practice will boost confidence and ensure smooth performances. Set aside some time for rehearsals, offering support and encouragement. It's all about having fun, not achieving perfection.

4. **Stage Set-Up:** Transform your living room into a vibrant performance space. Drape some sheets as curtains, gather pillows for an audience "seating area," and dim the lights for a dramatic effect. Get creative with decorations and props.

5. **Showtime:** Let the performances begin. Designate a family member as the MC, introducing each act with flair and encouraging the audience to cheer loudly. Here, enthusiasm is crucial.

6. **Award Silly Prizes:** After each act, shower the performers with silly prizes. The funnier, the better. Award categories like "Most Creative," "Most Enthusiastic," or "Most Likely to Go Viral." Let laughter and silly awards be the highlight, not competition.

7. **Celebration Time:** Once all the acts are complete, celebrate the amazing talent (and courage) displayed. Take photos, capture videos, and reminisce about the funniest moments. Make it a night to remember.

Benefits:

- **Boosts Confidence:** Stepping outside your comfort zone and performing in front of loved ones will do wonders for self-confidence. It teaches kids (and adults) to embrace their individuality and celebrate their unique talents.

- **Strengthens Family Bond:** Working together towards a common goal, sharing laughter, and cheering each other on fosters a strong family connection and creates lasting memories.

- **Sparks Creativity and Expression:** This activity encourages imagination, creativity, and the freedom to express oneself uniquely. It's a fun outlet for everyone to tap into their inner artist and performers.

- **Unforgettable Fun:** This activity guarantees to bring laughter, silly moments, and heartwarming memories that will be cherished for years.

Ditch the screens, gather your family, and unleash your inner superstars. The goal is to have fun, be creative, and celebrate each other's unique talents (or lack thereof). Get ready for a night filled with laughter, applause, and unforgettable family moments. The curtain is about to rise on your very own Family Talent Show.

Activity 40: Painting Projects

Spending time as a family can be a heartwarming experience, but sometimes, it's hard to find the perfect activity to bring everyone together. Painting projects could be ideal if you want a fun and creative way to bond with your family. Whether you are an experienced artist or a beginner, painting can be a relaxing and entertaining activity for everyone in your family. This section will explore some painting project ideas you can do with your family and unleash your inner artist.

Painting can be a relaxing activity for all family members.

Materials Needed

Before starting on any painting projects, you will need to gather a few items:

- Paint brushes that are appropriate for the size of the canvas you plan to use
- A canvas or a sturdy board to paint on
- A palette to mix your colors
- Paint. Acrylic paints can be a great choice due to their quick-drying properties
- A jar of fresh water for cleaning brushes

Step-by-Step Instructions

Here are some simple steps to follow when starting a painting project with your family:

1. Choose a subject, such as a landscape or a portrait. You can also use stencils or tracing paper to create outlines before painting.
2. Lay down some old newspapers to protect your surroundings.
3. Mix the paints on your palette and prime your brushes with water to clean them.
4. Finally, start painting and experiment with colors and textures. You can even try some three-dimensional elements like glitter or sand.

Additional Ideas

There are many ways to make painting projects enjoyable and inspiring for your family. For example, you could try the following:

- Collaborating on a single painting
- Painting on unconventional surfaces like rocks, shoes, or recycled materials
- Creating a mural that each family member contributes to
- Hosting a painting contest that awards prizes for creativity or originality

Painting projects are a fantastic way to ignite your family's creativity, bring everyone closer together, and produce a beautiful piece of art. With these simple steps and some basic materials, you can have a fun-filled afternoon while creating a masterpiece you can all be proud of. It doesn't matter if you are a seasoned artist or a beginner; painting projects are a great way to express yourself and explore new ideas. But remember, the most important thing is to have fun and enjoy the experience together as a family!

Activity 41: Recycled Fashion Show

Are you tired of the usual family game nights? Craving an activity that sparks the imagination, embraces sustainability, and results in side-splitting laughter? Look no further than a Recycled Fashion Show. This unique event combines fashion design, eco-awareness, and friendly competition, creating memories that will last long after the final strut down the runway. **Materials Needed:**

- Recycled materials: newspapers, plastic bags, cardboard, fabric scraps, aluminum foil, anything goes.
- Scissors, tape, glue, and staplers
- Paints, markers, and other decorating supplies (optional)
- Empty boxes, chairs, or blankets to create a makeshift runway (optional)
- Silly props and accessories (optional)

• Prizes for "Most Creative," "Most Outrageous," and "Most Funniest" designs (optional)

Step-by-Step Instructions:

1. **Theme Time:** Decide on a fun theme for your fashion show, like "Ocean Odyssey," "Galactic Glam," or "Superhero Showdown." It will inspire your designs and add a layer of excitement.

2. **Design and Build:** Let imaginations run wild. Transform newspapers into flowing gowns, plastic bags into shimmering scales, and cardboard into sturdy armor. Encourage everyone to use their unique talents and styles.

3. **Accessorize and Embellish:** Add finishing touches with paint, markers, sequins, buttons, or anything else that catches your fancy. Don't forget the power of silly props and accessories to elevate your outfit.

4. **Runway Ready:** Create a makeshift runway using chairs, blankets, or even an empty hallway. Get ready for the spotlight with catchy music and enthusiastic announcers (family members, of course).

5. **Strike a Pose:** Show off your creations with confidence and flair. Strut your stuff, twirl, and pose for the "family judges" (who get to award those fun prizes, remember?).

6. **Celebrate Sustainability:** After the final catwalk, take a moment to appreciate the amazing designs created entirely from recycled materials. Discuss the importance of sustainability and how even small actions make a difference.

Benefits:

- **Boosts Creativity and Imagination:** Encourages families to think outside the box and utilize everyday materials uniquely.

- **Promotes Sustainability:** Raises awareness about the importance of recycling and reusing materials, fostering eco-conscious habits.

- **Builds Teamwork and Communication:** Requires families to collaborate on designs and support each other during the creation process.

- **Sparks Laughter and Fun:** Provides a lighthearted and engaging activity that will have everyone giggling and creating silly memories.

- **Strengthens Family Bond:** Creates a shared experience that fosters connection and understanding between family members.

Forget expensive costumes and fast fashion. A Recycled Fashion Show is all about embracing creativity, having fun, and celebrating sustainability with the people you love. Gather your recyclables, unleash your inner fashionistas, and get ready for a catwalk extravaganza that's sure to be anything but ordinary. The most important accessory is a big smile and a heart full of imagination.

Activity 42: Movie-Making Marathon

Have you ever wished to step onto the silver screen and create a cinematic masterpiece? Well, dust off your director's hat, gather your family crew and get ready for a thrilling adventure in filmmaking. A family movie-making marathon is the perfect way to unleash creativity, bond over a shared project, and end up with hilarious (and potentially award-winning) results. Grab your popcorn, dim the lights, and start rolling.

Materials Needed:

- Smartphones, tablets, or a basic video camera
- Tripod (optional, but highly recommended)
- Costumes, props, and set decorations (get creative with household items)
- Writing materials for your script
- Editing software (simple, free options are available online)
- Enthusiasm and a sprinkle of imagination

Step-by-Step Instructions:

1. **Theme Time:** Gather your family and brainstorm. Choose a fun genre to inspire your movie, like comedy, sci-fi, mystery, or even a superhero adventure. The possibilities are endless.
2. **Script and Storyboard:** It's time to become screenwriters. Collaborate on a short script, even if it's just a few pages. Create a storyboard to visually plan your scenes.
3. **Lights, Camera, Action:** Grab your camera and start filming. Assign roles within your family (actors, directors, camerapersons, sound technicians) and get creative with filming angles and shots. Don't worry about perfection, embrace the bloopers and have fun.
4. **Editing Magic:** Once you've filmed your scenes, it's time to edit. Use simple editing software to put your movie together, add music and sound effects, and create your masterpiece.
5. **Premiere Night:** Roll out the red carpet (or a blanket on the living room floor) and host a premiere night for your family and friends. Showcase your creation, enjoy some popcorn, and bask in the applause (and laughter).

Benefits:

- **Boosts Creativity and Imagination:** Encourages everyone to think outside the box and work together to bring a story to life.
- **Strengthens Family Bond:** Creates a shared experience that fosters communication, collaboration, and problem-solving skills.
- **Develops Technical Skills:** Introduces families to basic filmmaking techniques and editing software in a fun and engaging way.

A family movie-making marathon is more than just creating a film. It's about creating memories, laughter, and a sense of accomplishment together. Grab your cameras, unleash your inner Spielbergs, and get ready to yell "Action!" Who knows, your next blockbuster might just come from your living room.

Activity 43: Photography Challenges

With a camera and a few prompts, you can awaken your inner photographer and capture some fantastic memories. Suppose you're still trying to figure out where to start. In that case, we've got you covered with step-by-step instructions and additional ideas to inspire your creativity.

Materials Needed

- A camera (phone camera, point-and-shoot, or DSLR)
- A timer (optional)

- A list of prompts (see below for ideas)

Step-by-Step Instructions

1. Choose a prompt from the list below.
2. Set up your camera and timer (if using).
3. Take turns capturing photos that fit the prompt. You can interpret the prompt as creatively as you like.
4. Review your photos and choose your favorites.
5. Share your photos and discuss what you like about them.

Prompts:

- Self-portrait
- Something that makes you happy
- A shadow
- A pattern
- Something blue
- A close-up of nature
- A silhouette
- Something that represents family

Additional Ideas

- Turn your photo challenge into a scavenger hunt by hiding objects that fit the prompts and having family members find and photograph them.
- Make a time-lapse video by taking a photo every few seconds for a set amount of time.
- Print out your favorite photos and create a family photo album or wall display.

Photography challenges are a fun and creative way to spend time with family while capturing memories. With just a camera and some prompts, you can snap some fantastic photos you'll cherish for years.

From collages to murals, weaving to sculpture-making, there are endless possibilities for artistic exploration. So, let your imagination run wild as you pick up paintbrushes, cameras, and other tools to bring your ideas to life. And remember the thrill of a family art scavenger hunt, where you can uncover hidden gems and use them as inspiration for your next project. With these activities, you'll create beautiful pieces and strengthen bonds with your children.

Chapter 5: Revamping Game Night

If you're tired of the same old game night routine with your family, it's time to revamp it and bring some excitement back. With an open mind and a little creativity, you can turn your mundane game nights into memorable experiences that your loved ones will treasure. The key is offering various games, inventive variations on classic games, and new activities to keep everyone engaged.

This chapter will help you think outside the box and mix the types of games you usually play. It'll take you beyond the classic board games and introduce you to unique and unfamiliar games that are still fun for children and adults. You'll also find tips on creating a welcoming environment, fostering healthy competition, and promoting sportsmanship. The goal is to make game nights something your family looks forward to and cherishes.

Inventive Variations on Classic Games

Game nights with family can become monotonous and boring if you always stick to the same old games. Here are some inventive variations on classic games to add to the mix and take your family game night to the next level. From themed elements to DIY games, these new twists excite and spark your game night. So, grab your family and favorite board games, and let's play.

Revamping classic board games can make them more interesting for all family members.

Activity 44: One-Word Story

Start with a single word, like "door." Each person adds one word, building a story sentence by sentence. You might end up with a thrilling adventure, a heartwarming tale, or a nonsensical yet hilarious journey. This simple game fosters creativity, listening skills, and unexpected twists.

Example:

- Player 1: Door
- Player 2: Creaks
- Player 3: Open
- Player 4: Revealing...

See where the story takes you!

Activity 45: Storytelling Dice Game

Create your own dice with prompts like characters (pirate, detective, astronaut), settings (castle, jungle, spaceship), and actions (runs away, solves a riddle, falls in love). Players roll the dice and create a collaborative story based on the results. This game is perfect for fostering imagination, improvisation, and teamwork.

Example:

- Player 1 rolls: Detective, Jungle, Climbs a Tree
- Player 2: "Our detective, lost in the dense jungle, must climb a towering tree to escape a pack of hungry monkeys."
- Player 3: "But as he reaches the top, he spots a hidden temple ruins..."

What adventures await next?

Activity 46: Blind Taste Test

Blindfold participants and have them taste different foods or drinks. Can they guess the ingredients and origin? This game is a fun way to explore new flavors, challenge preconceptions, and appreciate the complexity of taste.

Example:

- Food/Drink: Dark chocolate with chili flakes
- Player 1: "Hmm, I taste something sweet and spicy... maybe cinnamon and peppers?"
- Player 2: "I get a hint of bitterness too... could it be coffee with chili flakes?"
- Player 3: "Maybe dark chocolate with something savory... like bacon?"

Who has the most discerning palate?

Activity 47: Bringing Playwrights to the Party

Another creative way to revive your usual game night is to elevate it with some improvisational plays. Take turns being the host and set up scenarios on a game board. You can create storylines and character roles around the board. So, for example, in the game Scrabble, players can invent and act out a scene from a play using the words they've spelled.

Activity 48: Switching It Up

Finally, one of the simplest ways to refresh game night is to switch up the games and select a new game every week. Consider taking family polls to help come up with ideas. Depending on preference or play style, you can even have each family member play a different game. The idea is to keep the momentum going and maintain an element of surprise.

Family game nights are a time-honored tradition, but there's no reason it has to be boring. When you add a touch of imagination and creativity, you can reinvent classic games to make them fun and exciting. By mixing in themed elements, creating unique DIY games, hosting a family tournament, or even improvising some playwrights, you can ensure that game night will be a delightful and memorable evening for everyone.

Unique and Unfamiliar Games

It's game night with the family. Let's face it: we all want something new and exciting. With a library full of board and card games at home, it's easy to slip into a routine of always playing the same handful of games with loved ones. However, it's time to shake things up and overhaul game night with some unique and unfamiliar games. This section explores different categories of games that are just as fun but less familiar to you and your family. So, whether you're looking for a cozy night at home or a thrill-filled evening with your family, try out these exciting, non-digital games that will bring everyone closer together.

Activity 49: Artistic Games

Are you looking for a creative outlet for your family game night? Try out Pictionary, in which you must guess drawings made by others. Or unravel twisted tales with Dixit, where players create their stories and blend their imaginations to think of the right card.

Activity 50: Verbal Games

Oral games are perfect if you enjoy more personal games. These games challenge you to share secrets and push you out of your comfort zone, making them delightful and engaging. For example, in "Never Have I Ever," each player takes a turn stating something they have never done before, and if another player has done it, they take a sip of water or any beverage of their choice.

Activity 51: Musical Charades

Ditch the charades charades and express yourself through music. Hum, sing, or dance out movie titles, books, or even emotions. Challenge yourselves with different genres or instruments for added difficulty. This game is perfect for music lovers, party nights, and unleashing hidden talents.

Example:

- Theme: Sci-Fi Movie
- Player 1: Sings the iconic theme song from Star Wars
- Player 2: Dances a robotic jig representing Terminator
- Player 3: Humms the suspenseful theme from Alien

Can you guess the movie?

Activity 52: Roleplaying Games

Roleplaying games are the perfect fit for an innovative and interactive experience. Fans of Harry Potter can try their hands on Hogwarts Battle, while Game of Thrones followers could indulge in A Game of Thrones: The Board Game. These games are challenging and require multiple players to engage and work together.

Activity 53: Escape Room Games

The exit from the scary room with time ticking down adds a rush to the game, making it one of the most thrilling cooperative games out there. Escape rooms typically involve puzzles and riddles that players must figure out how to "escape" within the given time. Some ideas include The Heist and Escape from Atlantis.

Activity 54: Trivia Games

Trivia games make for a fun-filled and competitive night with your family. You can pick topics like history, music, sports, or pop culture and test each other's knowledge with games like Trivial Pursuit or Smart Ass. If you're looking for a unique twist, consider Quizizz or Kahoot!, which are games played on mobile devices.

Activity 55: Blindfolded Pictionary

One person draws a picture blindfolded while their partner describes it. The result? Hilarious misinterpretations and creative problem-solving. This game is perfect for large groups, laughter, and testing your communication skills.

Example:

- Player 1 (drawing): Scribbles furiously while blindfolded
- Player 2 (describing): "Okay, I see a circle... with, uh, something long coming out of it... and maybe a squiggle on top?"
- Player 1: Draws more lines and dots
- Player 2: "Hmmm... could it be a giraffe wearing a hat?"

Will they guess the right answer?

Your family game night doesn't have to be dull and monotonous, with the same tired board games or card games day after day. Instead, try out different game genres with your loved ones to create unforgettable memories. Whether trivia games, escape room games, or classic board games, the possibilities are endless, and the experiences can be upbeat and great fun. So, the next time you plan a family game night, pick an unfamiliar game and have fun trying it out with your loved ones.

Creating a Fun Atmosphere

Do you remember those game nights from your childhood? Chances are, you have fond memories of spending quality time with friends and family. However, with the advancement of technology, we spend less time connecting with loved ones in person. That is why revamping game night with family is a great way to bring everyone together and create lasting memories. But how do you make the experience more enjoyable?

Establishing Ground Rules

Everyone must know the rules before starting a game. Establishing the rules before the game begins prevents confusion and avoids disputes. Ensure that everyone understands the game's objective, how to score, and any other important rules.

Encouraging Good Sportsmanship

Good sportsmanship is essential for a fun family game night. Encourage your family to be gracious winners and good losers. Remind everyone that the objective is to have fun and spend quality time with one another, not compete. However, no one likes a sore loser, so everyone must practice respect, even amid defeat.

Keeping Score

It's important to keep score during game night, but it's equally important to maintain a healthy perspective on the score. Remember that the game score is not a reflection of personal abilities or worth but rather a measure of how well everyone played, which includes a bit of chance.

Creating an Engaging Environment

Creating a festive ambiance during game night will help everyone feel more relaxed and in good spirits. Decorate the game area with festive tablecloths and balloons. Light candles and play some feel-good tunes in the background. Another way to enhance the game atmosphere is by creating a special game night snack or potluck.

Revamping game night with family is a fantastic way to bond and create lasting memories. By establishing ground rules, encouraging good sportsmanship, keeping score, and creating an engaging environment, you will indeed have a game night to remember. So have fun and enjoy making new memories with loved ones.

Making It Memorable

Family game nights create opportunities for families to have fun, bond, and create lasting memories. But, whether you're a family of four or a more prolific family, there is a way to make the game night even more special. In this section, you'll find ideas on revamping game night to make it more memorable.

Creating Traditions

Start by creating a tradition. A tradition instills a sense of belonging and provides a sense of continuity in our unpredictable world. You might think you don't have any family traditions, but you'll be surprised at how many you already have. For example, does your family always eat nachos during game night? Do you have a specific game that everyone loves to play? These little things, when done consistently, become traditions. Consider incorporating new things, such as having everyone wear matching team shirts or having a themed game night.

Sharing Stories and Playing Music

Playing music and sharing stories are great ways to make the game night memorable. You can create a playlist of your family's favorite songs during game night. This will bring back memories and create new ones. For stories, each family member can share a fun or interesting story. This activity can create good laughter and improve communication skills.

Celebrating Victories

Whenever someone wins a game, celebrate their victory. You can create a team cheer or have everyone give high-fives to the winning team. Celebrating successes generates a positive atmosphere and makes everyone feel good about themselves. Adding prizes or rewards to game night can make it even more fun. Get creative with your tips. They don't have to be expensive.

Taking Photos/Videos

Lastly, take lots of photos and videos. These are great memories that you can have forever. You can print them out and put them into albums or make a family game night scrapbook. Then, years later, you can look back at those memories and reminisce about the good times. The videos can also be shared with relatives and friends who couldn't make it to game night.

Making game night more memorable is all about having fun and being creative. With the tips set out, you can ensure that game night is an experience your family will never forget. The game night should be enjoyable and stress-free, so remember to take lots of breaks and stay positive. Most of all, appreciate the time you have with your family and enjoy the moment.

Chapter 6: Cooking and Baking as a Family

One way to bond with your family is by cooking and baking together. In today's fast-paced world, it's getting more and more difficult to carve out precious moments where you can connect, and as everyone has to eat, cooking together is ideal. In addition, it's an excellent way to cultivate a love for food and the art of cooking. There's something magical about combining different ingredients, flavors, and textures to create something delectable. Whether teaching your kids how to make cookies or whipping up a delicious meal for dinner, cooking and baking as a family is a bonding experience everyone will cherish forever.

This chapter will explore five activities and recipes to strengthen family connections. From creating a family recipe book to making cupcakes, these activities will inspire creativity and bring out the best in each family member. With age-appropriate tasks and safety precautions, you can ensure everyone is having a good time while learning, exploring, and enjoying a delicious meal!

Activity 56: Create a Family Recipe Book

Creating a family recipe book can bring back childhood memories.
https://unsplash.com/photos/0S2rRstB_9M

Food is an essential part of every family. We all have that one recipe that has been passed down from generation to generation, and even when we grow up and start our own families, we still hold on to these family recipes. The taste of traditional dishes always brings back memories of our childhood, family get-togethers, and holidays. That's why creating a family recipe book is an excellent idea to keep these delicious treasures safe for generations.

Materials Needed:

- Recipe Collection: Gather all your family's cherished handwritten and printed recipes.
- Blank Recipe Book or Binder: Choose a durable book or binder with enough pages to accommodate all the recipes.
- Dividers or Tabs: Use these to categorize recipes, such as appetizers, main dishes, desserts, etc.
- Recipe Cards: If you prefer a more interactive approach, use blank recipe cards for handwritten entries.
- Pens, Markers, and Art Supplies: These will come in handy if you want to add personal touches and decorations.
- Scanners or Photocopiers: These can be useful for digitizing old handwritten recipes.
- Camera or Smartphone: For capturing appetizing photos of the prepared dishes.
- Family Members' Input: Reach out to family members for additional recipes and anecdotes.
- Computer and Printer: If you're planning to include digital recipes or typed stories.

Step-by-Step Instructions:

1. Recipe Gathering: Collect recipes from family members. This can include traditional favorites, special occasion dishes, and those with heartwarming stories.
2. Sort and Categorize: Organize recipes into categories like breakfast, appetizers, main courses, desserts, and drinks. Use dividers or tabs to separate these sections.
3. Record Family Stories: Alongside each recipe, add a brief backstory or memory associated with it. This adds a personal touch and makes the book even more special.
4. Personalize the Pages: If using a blank recipe book or binder, write or type the recipes on the pages. If using recipe cards, encourage family members to handwrite their contributions.
5. Include Photographs: Add pictures of the finished dishes for visual appeal. These photos can evoke fond memories and make the book more engaging.
6. Decorate Creatively: If desired, use markers, stickers, or art supplies to decorate the pages. You can create a unified theme or let each recipe have its unique design.
7. Digitize and Preserve: Consider scanning or photocopying handwritten recipes to ensure their preservation. You can add digital versions to the book or store them separately.
8. Family Contributions: Invite family members to contribute their recipes and memories, making the book a collaborative effort.
9. Test and Adapt: Prepare a few recipes from the book to ensure accuracy and taste. Adjust instructions if needed and note any variations.

Benefits:

- Preservation of Traditions: Family recipes carry the essence of generations and cultures, preserving them for years.

- Legacy for Generations: A recipe book is a tangible legacy to pass on to future generations, ensuring they can savor the flavors of the past.

Creating a family recipe book is like crafting a culinary tapestry that weaves together flavors, memories, and stories. As you compile these treasured recipes, you're not just creating a cookbook. You're preserving a piece of your family's history and sharing a timeless gift with future generations. From the handwritten notes of a beloved grandparent to the carefully documented secrets of a special dish, your family recipe book will become a cherished heirloom that nourishes the body and soul, one recipe at a time.

Themed Dinner Nights

Cooking and baking with your family is a way to bond and create memories and an opportunity to teach essential life skills like organization, patience, and teamwork. Hosting themed dinner nights is a fun way to make the experience even more enjoyable. It lets you get creative in the kitchen and is a fun activity for the whole family. This section discusses different themed dinner night ideas and how to make the experience successful.

Activity 57: Taco Night

This theme is perfect for any family who loves Mexican food. You could set up a toppings bar with different meats, beans, and veggies and let everyone build their own tacos. You can even make homemade tortillas and salsa to take the meal to the next level. Remember to create a festive atmosphere by playing some lively Latin music and decorating the table with sombreros and colorful tablecloths.

Activity 58: Italian Night

Who doesn't love a big, hearty bowl of pasta? You can get creative with different sauces and pasta shapes with Italian Night. You can also make appetizers like bruschetta or Caprese salad. To make it even more fun, play some Italian tunes and have everyone dress up in red, white, and green.

Activity 59: Breakfast Dinner Night

Breakfast for dinner? Yes, please! This theme is perfect for any family who loves brunch. You can make sweet dishes like pancakes or waffles – or savory dishes like omelets. For an added touch, decorate the table with flowers and use fancy plates and silverware.

Activity 60: BBQ Night

This theme is perfect for any summertime gathering. Fire up the grill and make burgers, hotdogs, and ribs. You can also make sides like mac and cheese or baked beans. Set up some lawn games like cornhole or frisbee to make it even more fun.

Activity 61: Japanese Night

Sushi, anyone? Japanese Night is perfect for families that love Asian cuisine. You can make sushi rolls, dumplings, and rice bowls. For an added touch, decorate the table with chopsticks and paper lanterns. You can also play some traditional Japanese music to set the mood.

Themed dinner nights are a fun and creative way to bond with your family in the kitchen. With so many different themes, there is something for every family's taste. Remember to get the whole family involved in the planning process to make it even more of a bonding experience. Remember to take pictures and create lasting memories!

Activity 62: Bake and Decorate Desserts

Sharing a common interest like cooking and baking can bring your family together and create an enjoyable way to connect. One fun activity you can include in your family's cooking and baking routine is decorating desserts. Not only is it a great way to spend time together, but it also allows for creativity and personal expression. Here's everything you need to know for baking and decorating desserts with your family.

Materials Needed:

- Baking Ingredients: Flour, sugar, eggs, butter, and any specific ingredients for your chosen dessert.
- Baking Tools: Mixing bowls, measuring cups and spoons, electric mixer, spatulas, baking pans, and parchment paper.
- Decorating Supplies: Frosting, icing bags and tips, food coloring, sprinkles, edible glitter, chocolate chips, fruit slices, and other decorative items.
- Aprons and Towels: Keep things mess-free and comfortable by donning aprons and having towels on hand.
- Recipe: Choose a dessert recipe that suits your family's preferences and skill level.
- Camera: Capture the creative process and the final masterpiece.

Step-by-Step Instructions:

1. Select a Recipe: Choose a dessert recipe that suits your family's taste and skill level. It could be cookies, cupcakes, a cake, or even a more intricate pastry.
2. Gather Ingredients: Collect all the necessary ingredients and tools to ensure a smooth baking process.
3. Preparation: Preheat the oven as per the recipe instructions. Assemble all the ingredients and utensils on the countertop for easy access.
4. Mix and Bake: Involve everyone in measuring and mixing the ingredients according to the recipe. Let each family member take turns to contribute.
5. Baking Time: Pop the dessert into the oven and use this time to discuss the decorating plans or engage in a fun kitchen-related game.
6. Cooling Phase: Once the dessert is baked, allow it to cool completely before moving on to decorating.
7. Decorating Delights: Set up a decorating station with an array of frosting, icing colors, sprinkles, and other decorative items. Let each family member's creativity shine as they adorn the desserts.
8. Themed Creations: Consider choosing a theme for your dessert decorations. It could be seasonal (like Halloween or Christmas), based on a favorite movie or book, or just a burst of colorful creativity.

Benefits:

- Creativity: Decorating desserts lets each family member express their unique creativity and style.
- Life Skills: Children learn valuable kitchen skills, from measuring ingredients to mastering basic techniques.

By including decorating desserts as part of your cooking routine, your family can enjoy creativity and personal expression while learning valuable skills. Remember to have fun, be patient with one another, and celebrate your successes together. Creating meaningful memories in the kitchen is a gift your family will cherish for years.

Activity 63: DIY Pizza Bars

Imagine a scene where your family gathers around a table filled with a colorful array of toppings, sauce, cheese, and dough. The air is filled with laughter and anticipation as each family member embarks on a culinary adventure to design their perfect pizza. DIY pizza bars offer a delightful experience along with a chance for creativity and bonding.

Materials Needed:

- Pizza Dough: Pre-made or homemade dough, depending on your preference.
- Sauce Selection: Tomato sauce, pesto, white sauce, or any other preferred base.
- Cheese Variety: Mozzarella, cheddar, parmesan, and more.
- Toppings Galore: A variety of vegetables (bell peppers, mushrooms, onions, olives, etc.), meats (pepperoni, sausage, ham, etc.), and herbs (basil, oregano, etc.).
- Cooking Tools: Baking sheets or pizza stones, rolling pin, pizza cutter, spatula.
- Dipping Sauces: Optional, but adding a selection of dipping sauces like marinara, garlic butter, or ranch can enhance the experience.
- Aprons and Chef Hats: To create a festive and engaging atmosphere.

Step-by-Step Instructions:

1. Preparation Stage: Set up a spacious area where everyone can access the toppings easily. Lay out all the ingredients, sauces, and cheese in separate bowls.

2. Roll Out the Dough: If using pre-made dough, follow the package instructions for rolling it out. If making your own, get ready-rolled dough or prepare it in advance.

3. Sauce Spreading: Provide spoons for each family member to spread their choice of sauce over their pizza base. Remind them that the sauce is the canvas upon which they'll build their masterpiece.

4. Cheese Adventure: Let the cheese layer commence! Encourage everyone to sprinkle their preferred cheese generously over their sauced dough.

5. Top It Off: This is where the creativity shines. Each family member can design their pizza with an assortment of toppings. From classic combinations to adventurous creations, let imaginations run wild.

6. Into the Oven: Once the pizzas are dressed to perfection, transfer them onto baking sheets or pizza stones and place them in a preheated oven. Follow the dough's baking instructions for a golden crust.

7. Dip and Delight: While the pizzas bake, set out an array of dipping sauces to accompany the final product.

Benefits:

- Customization: Everyone gets to design their pizza according to their taste and preferences.

- Collaboration: Working together in the kitchen fosters teamwork and a shared accomplishment.

Creating a DIY pizza bar turns an ordinary meal into an exciting culinary adventure. It's a unique opportunity to blend flavors, experiment with toppings, and, most importantly, bond as a family over a shared activity. From shaping the dough to selecting toppings and watching the pizzas bake, each step is an expression of creativity and unity!

Activity 64: Fun Cupcakes

Making cupcakes as a family can be an enjoyable experience.
Photo by Brooke Lark https://unsplash.com/photos/six-teal-icing-cupcakes-with-sprinkles-pGM4sjt_BdQ?utm_content=creditCopyText&utm_medium=referral&utm_source=unsplash

In the realm of sweet treats, cupcakes hold a special place. The allure of these miniature cakes lies in their delectable taste and the joy of baking them together as a family. Whether you're a seasoned baker or just starting your culinary journey, creating cupcakes can transform an ordinary afternoon into a delightful adventure.

Materials Needed:

- Cupcake Ingredients: Flour, sugar, eggs, butter, baking powder, vanilla extract, milk, and any additional flavors or mix-ins.
- Mixing Bowls and Utensils: Bowls, spoons, measuring cups, and a hand mixer for efficient mixing.

- Cupcake Liners: Colorful and festive cupcake liners to add flair to your creations.
- Baking Pans: Use a cupcake or muffin tin to hold the batter while baking.
- Frosting and Decorations: Various types of frosting (buttercream, cream cheese, etc.), food coloring, piping bags, and decorating tips.
- Toppings: Sprinkles, chocolate chips, fruit, edible glitter, and any other creative toppings your family enjoys.
- Aprons and Oven Mitts: For a touch of baking style and safety.

Step-by-Step Instructions:

1. Gather Ingredients: Assemble all the necessary ingredients and materials in a clean and organized workspace. Put on your aprons and get ready to dive into the baking adventure.
2. Mix the Batter: Depending on your chosen recipe, combine the dry and wet ingredients in separate bowls. Then, slowly incorporate the wet mixture into the dry ingredients until you have a smooth batter.
3. Line the Pans: Place colorful cupcake liners in the cupcake/muffin tins. This adds a decorative touch and makes it easier to remove the cupcakes after baking.
4. Fill the Liners: Using a spoon or ice cream scoop, fill each cupcake liner with the batter until they're about two-thirds full. This allows room for the cupcakes to rise.
5. Bake to Perfection: Preheat your oven to the temperature specified in your recipe. Carefully place the cupcake pans in the oven and bake according to the recipe's instructions.
6. Cool and Frost: Once the cupcakes are baked and golden, remove them from the oven and let them cool completely on a wire rack. While waiting, prepare your choice of frosting.
7. Decorate with Flair: This is where the fun truly begins. Set up a decorating station with an assortment of frostings, toppings, and decorations. Let each family member unleash their creativity and decorate their cupcakes as they please.

Benefits:

- Bonding Time: Baking as a family fosters connection and shared experiences.
- Skill Development: Children learn basic baking techniques and kitchen safety.

Baking fun cupcakes together is more than a culinary activity. It's a delightful way to nurture family bonds and create lasting memories. From mixing ingredients to artistic decoration, every step becomes an opportunity to laugh, learn, and express creativity!

This chapter discussed five easy ways to make cooking and baking a happy, bonding family time. A unique recipe accompanies each activity so you can create something special together. From creating a family recipe book to baking and decorating cupcakes, these activities will bring your family closer together and create lasting memories.

Chapter 7: Sharing and Creating Stories

Sharing stories with family is a memorable, one-and-only family experience that can bring you closer together and create lasting bonds. Whether it's sharing your personal experiences or creating new stories together, storytelling allows us to connect on a deeper level and better understand each other's perspectives. In addition, it's a chance to step away from the hustle and bustle of daily life and take a moment to reflect, reminisce, and appreciate all that we have accomplished and overcome as a family.

Sharing stories with family can bring you closer together.

Activity 65: Family Story Circle Sessions

Amidst the whirlwind of our modern lives, where time often slips through our fingers, the essence of family bonding can sometimes fade into the background. However, there exists a timeless tradition that has the power to reignite these connections and create treasured memories: storytelling. Gathering as a family to share stories, whether they're personal anecdotes or snippets from the past, has the magical ability to forge unbreakable bonds.

Materials Needed:

- Comfortable Seating: Arrange a cozy space with ample seating for everyone to sit comfortably.
- Mementos and Photos: Gather photo albums, family heirlooms, and mementos that might spark storytelling.
- Writing Materials: Provide notebooks and pens for those who wish to jot down story ideas.

Step-by-Step Instructions:

1. Set the Mood: Choose a relaxing and distraction-free environment for your Family Story Circle Session. Dim the lights, light some candles, or sit by a crackling fire to create an inviting atmosphere.

2. Create a Safe Space: Emphasize that this is a judgment-free zone. Encourage everyone to be open, honest, and vulnerable while sharing their stories.

3. Rotate Storytellers: Begin with a storyteller, perhaps the eldest or youngest family member, who shares a personal story, memory, or anecdote. After each story, rotate to the next family member.

4. Prompt Ideas: To kick off the session, you can use prompts like "Share a memorable childhood adventure" or "Tell us about a family tradition that warms your heart."

5. Listen and Engage: As each family member shares, listen attentively, offering supportive nods, smiles, and laughter where appropriate.

6. Build Upon Stories: Encourage family members to build upon one another's stories. This collaborative element can lead to unexpected twists and turns.

7. Laughter and Tears: Embrace the full spectrum of emotions, from hearty laughter to poignant tears. These shared feelings create deeper connections.

8. Capture the Moments: If desired, designate someone to jot down highlights or takeaways from each story session.

Benefits:

- Strengthened Bonds: Sharing personal narratives fosters understanding and empathy among family members.
- Cultural Legacy: Passing down family stories preserves your cultural and familial heritage for future generations.

Family Story Circle Sessions transcend generations, cultures, and time, uniting family members in a timeless tradition of connection. Through shared laughter, nostalgic tears, and the exchange of personal narratives, these sessions create an environment where every voice matters.

Activity 66: Memory Sharing and Recording through Interviews

Memories are the threads of your past that shape the fabric of your present and future. These cherished recollections hold the key to understanding who you are, where you come from, and the values that guide you. While the task of preserving these memories might seem daunting, the rewards are immeasurable. The art of memory sharing through intimate interviews with family members is a time-honored method to record and safeguard these invaluable narratives.

Materials Needed:

- Recording Device: Use a digital recorder, smartphone, or video camera to capture interviews.
- Notebook and Pen: Keep a notebook handy for jotting down questions, notes, and insights.
- Comfortable Space: Choose a cozy setting where the interviewee feels relaxed and open.
- Photo Albums and Mementos: Gather photos and mementos that can trigger memories during the interview.

Step-by-Step Instructions:

1. Select Interviewees: Begin by selecting family members you'd like to interview. Consider elders, parents, and other relatives with rich life experiences.

2. Choose a Focus: Decide on the theme or topics you want to explore during the interview. This could include childhood memories, significant life events, family traditions, and personal journeys.

3. Prepare Thoughtful Questions: Craft a list of open-ended questions that encourage storytelling. For example, "Tell me about a cherished family tradition" or "Can you recount a turning point in your life?"

4. Create a Comfortable Environment: Set the stage for a relaxed conversation. Ensure the interviewee is at ease and ready to share.

5. Begin with Warm-Up Questions: Start with light questions to establish rapport and help the interviewee ease into the process.

6. Listen Attentively: Listen actively, allowing the interviewee to lead the conversation. Encourage them to delve deeper into their stories.

7. Use Triggers: Share old photos, mementos, or family heirlooms to spark memories and prompt detailed narratives.

8. Follow the Flow: Let the conversation flow naturally. Your role is to guide and facilitate, not dominate the conversation.

9. Capture Emotions: Encourage the interviewee to express their emotions and feelings. These emotional nuances add depth to the recorded memories.

10. Embrace Silence: Don't be afraid of pauses or silence. Sometimes, the most profound reflections emerge in quiet moments.

11. Summarize and Reflect: At the end of the interview, summarize key points and ask the interviewee if they have any final thoughts to share.

Benefits:

- Emotional Connection: Hearing personal stories fosters emotional connections among family members.
- Legacy of Love: A recorded legacy to be passed down, ensuring the continuity of family narratives.

Through the art of memory sharing and recording interviews, you embark on a journey to unearth the treasures of your family's history. Each story shared is a glimpse into the essence of your family's journey through time. Capturing these narratives is an act of preserving the past for the benefit of the future. As you sit down with family members to unravel their memories, you're creating a legacy and strengthening the bonds that tie your family together!

Activity 67: Collaborative Story-Writing Projects

In a world overflowing with digital distractions, finding meaningful ways to bond as a family is a rewarding challenge. Collaborative story-writing projects unleash your family's collective creativity and weave stronger bonds among its members. This endeavor may appear daunting, but fear not! It's a captivating and innovative approach that promises joy, laughter, and the creation of memorable tales.

Materials Needed:

- Paper and Writing Tools: Stock up on paper, notebooks, or a shared digital document for story writing.
- Imagination and Open Minds: The most essential ingredients for crafting unique narratives.
- Willingness to Share: A spirit of openness and willingness to share ideas and thoughts.

Step-by-Step Instructions:

1. Set the Scene: Gather your family in a cozy and inspiring setting. This could be around the fireplace, in the backyard, or even on a virtual call.

2. Choose a Genre: Decide on a genre for your story. Will it be an adventure, mystery, fantasy, or something unique?

3. Initiate the Story: One person starts the story with a captivating opening sentence. This sets the stage for the tale to unfold.

4. Pass the Pen: Each family member takes turns contributing a sentence or a paragraph to the story. The story evolves with every new addition.

5. Build on Ideas: Embrace the unexpected twists and turns that others bring to the story. Build on their ideas and let the narrative take delightful detours.

6. Character Creation: Introduce characters to the story. Each family member can create and develop a character, complete with personalities and quirks.

7. Conflict and Resolution: Add conflict and obstacles to the story. Discuss as a family how the characters will overcome these challenges.

8. Use Your Senses: Encourage vivid descriptions that appeal to the senses. Transport readers into the story's world through rich imagery.

9. Keep It Flowing: Maintain the flow of the story by seamlessly transitioning from one family member's contribution to another's.

10. Don't Overthink: Embrace spontaneity and creativity. There's no need for perfection because the charm lies in the collaborative process.

11. Closure and Ending: As the story nears its conclusion, work together to craft a satisfying ending that wraps up the narrative.

12. Read Aloud: Once the story is complete, gather around and read the story aloud. Revel in the shared accomplishment and the tale you've woven together.

Benefits:

- Unleashing Creativity: Uncover hidden talents and explore the depths of your family's imagination.

- Shared Achievement: The completed story becomes a tangible reminder of your family's collaboration and creativity.

As you embark on collaborative story-writing projects, you venture into a realm where creativity knows no bounds and family bonds flourish. Each sentence crafted, every character introduced, and every twist added becomes a testament to the unity and shared creativity of your family. So, put aside the screens and remote controls and let your collective imagination guide you through the creation of unforgettable stories.

Activity 68: Fortunately, Unfortunately

Dive into the whimsical world of storytelling with the "Fortunately, Unfortunately" game. This creative activity encourages family members to collaborate on a story filled with unexpected twists and turns.

Step-by-Step Instructions:

1. Gather around: Sit in a circle or around a table where everyone can easily see and hear each other.

2. Start with "Fortunately": The first person begins the story with a sentence that starts with "Fortunately." For example, "Fortunately, the sun was shining brightly on the day of the big adventure."

3. Follow with "Unfortunately": The next person continues the story by adding a sentence that starts with "Unfortunately." For instance, "Unfortunately, a sudden storm cloud appeared out of nowhere."

4. Keep the pattern going: Family members take turns alternating between "fortunately" and "unfortunately" as they build the story. Each new sentence should react to the previous one, continuing the narrative.

5. Embrace the twists: Embrace the unexpected! As the story unfolds, you'll encounter delightful surprises and humorous contradictions.

6. Keep it going: Continue the back-and-forth pattern until you feel like the story has reached a satisfying conclusion.

Benefits:

- Creativity: Participants exercise their creativity by weaving a story together in real time, incorporating each other's contributions.

- Collaboration: Family members work together to create a cohesive narrative, learning to build upon each other's ideas.

"Fortunately, Unfortunately" is an entertaining way to experience storytelling as a dynamic and cooperative endeavor. As each participant adds their unique spin to the story, you'll witness the narrative take unexpected and delightful directions.

Activity 69: Word Association

Explore the depths of your family's imagination as you embark on a word association journey. This game is a fantastic way to weave a collective narrative while building connections between words.

Step-by-Step Instructions:

- Gather around: Sit in a circle or arrange yourselves comfortably so that everyone can hear each other.
- Begin with a word: The first person starts by saying a word aloud. It can be any word that comes to mind.
- Connect the dots: The next person responds with a word that is associated with the previous word. For instance, if the first word was "tree," the next word could be "leaves."
- Keep the chain going: Continue the pattern, with each family member responding to the previous word with a word that makes sense in relation to it.
- Explore tangents: As you progress, the words may take unexpected turns, leading to interesting and amusing associations.
- Avoid repetition: Try not to repeat words that have already been used in the game.

Benefits:

- Creativity: Participants exercise their creativity by quickly thinking of words that are related to the previous word.
- Vocabulary Building: The game encourages the use of a wide range of vocabulary, expanding everyone's word bank.

Word Association is a game that takes your family on a linguistic journey, exploring connections between words and discovering the unexpected paths they can lead to. It's a delightful way to foster creativity, language skills, and collaboration among family members.

Activity 70: Scene Building Improv

Unleash your family's inner actors and create hilarious scenes or scenarios with the "Scene Building Improv" exercise. This activity encourages spontaneous storytelling and provides a platform for endless laughter.

Step-by-Step Instructions:

1. Gather the ensemble: Assemble your family members in a comfortable space where everyone can see and hear each other.
2. Set the stage: Begin by announcing a simple scenario or setting, such as "at a bakery," "lost in the jungle," or "on a spaceship."
3. Choose characters: Each family member takes on a character role for the scene. Feel free to get creative. You can be a chef, an explorer, an alien, a talking animal, or anything your imagination conjures.

4. Start the scene: The scene begins with one family member initiating the interaction based on the scenario and their chosen character.

5. React and respond: As the scene progresses, each family member jumps in with their characters, reacting and responding to what's happening. There's no script. It's all about improvisation and spontaneity.

6. Keep the story alive: Continuously build on the story as characters interact, face challenges, and embark on adventures within the chosen setting.

7. Embrace surprises: Expect the unexpected! The charm of improv lies in the unexpected twists and turns that arise from everyone's contributions.

8. Keep the energy flowing: Encourage everyone to jump in and contribute, ensuring that the scene evolves dynamically.

Benefits:

- Laughter: The unpredictable nature of the activity often leads to hilarious situations and uproarious laughter.
- Communication Skills: Improv enhances communication skills by requiring active listening and effective interaction.

Scene Building Improv is a fantastic way to break the ice, encourage spontaneity, and bring a dose of lightheartedness to family gatherings. Through shared storytelling, you'll create memorable moments full of laughter and imagination.

Storytelling games, improv exercises, and collaborative writing projects are great ways to bring families closer together while fostering creativity, communication, and laughter. By preparing appropriately, establishing clear guidelines, and choosing suitable activities, families can create fun and memorable experiences that will enhance their relationships and strengthen their bonds for years to come.

Chapter 8: Activities for Fitness and Fun

Taking care of your family's health and building solid parent-child connections go hand in hand. As a parent, it's natural to want what's best for your children. It includes promoting healthy habits that will help them thrive physically and mentally. But the importance of fostering a positive relationship with your children often gets overlooked. Connecting with them and genuinely listening to their needs and concerns strengthens your bond and provides a safe space for them to grow and develop.

Benefits of Physical Activity for Families

Living a healthy family lifestyle can profoundly impact both parents and children. Regular physical activity improves our overall physical health, boosts our mood, reduces stress, and helps foster strong relationships with our loved ones. In addition, engaging in fitness activities with your kids shows you are setting an excellent example for them to follow and creating opportunities for parent-child bonding. Whether biking, hiking, or playing a game of catch, these activities offer the perfect opportunity for quality time and meaningful conversations.

Exercising with your children can help you create a strong parent-child bond.
https://www.pexels.com/photo/photo-of-girl-hugging-her-mom-while-doing-yoga-pose-4473612/

Safety and Adaptability Considerations

There's no reason to sacrifice fun and fitness for safety. Family activities that promote both can be the perfect solution. The possibilities are endless, from hiking and biking to outdoor scavenger hunts and backyard yoga sessions. The key is choosing engaging, challenging, enjoyable activities for everyone involved. Here are a few tips:

- Equip everyone with the right gear, such as helmets and proper footwear
- Ensure their safety by familiarizing yourself with the activity you plan to do and any potential hazards
- Allow for adaptability and flexibility so that everyone can participate at their own pace
- Consider the ages and abilities of each family member before choosing an activity

Activity 71: Cosmic Bowling

Transform your living room into a mini-bowling alley with simple materials and a sprinkle of creativity. The pulsating lights, the thumping music, and the satisfying strike of pins flying are a recipe for pure fun. It's a perfect activity for family game nights, birthday parties, or just a fun way to unwind after a long day. Dim the lights, crank up the tunes, and get ready to roll some strikes.

Materials Needed:

- **Bowling Essentials:** Bowling balls (traditional or lightweight), pins (glow-in-the-dark or decorated), or even empty water bottles as makeshift pins.
- **Lighting:** Blacklights, string lights, fairy lights, disco ball (optional) – get creative!
- **Alley Creation (optional):** Cardboard boxes, furniture, blankets, or any materials you can use to create a makeshift bowling lane.
- **Decorations (optional):** Glow sticks, streamers, posters – add some cosmic flair!
- **Music:** Upbeat tunes to set the mood.

Step-by-Step Instructions:

1. **Set the Scene:** Dim the lights or turn them off completely. Drape your chosen lighting around the room, focusing on the bowling area. If you're creating a makeshift lane, use boxes, furniture, or blankets to define the boundaries.
2. **Glow it up:** Decorate with glow sticks, streamers, or posters to create a cosmic ambiance. Encourage everyone to wear neon or glow-in-the-dark clothing for extra fun.
3. **Get Ready to Roll:** Choose your bowling balls and pins. If using water bottles, fill them with water and add glow sticks for an extra touch.
4. **Strike a Pose:** Crank up the music and get ready to bowl! Keep score as usual, or create your fun scoring system with bonus points for strikes or creative throws.
5. **Celebrate the Winners:** Don't forget to award prizes (real or imaginary) to the champions of the night!

Benefits:

- **Budget-friendly:** Save money on expensive bowling alley trips and enjoy the fun at home.

- **Customization:** Tailor the experience to your preferences. Choose your music, and decorations, and even create your unique bowling challenges.
- **Family Bonding:** Create lasting memories and laughter together as you bowl the night away.
- **Indoor Activity:** Perfect for rainy days or when you want to stay cozy indoors.
- **Promotes Physical Activity:** Bowling is a fun way to get some exercise and have a blast.

Ditch the traditional and embrace the cosmic. With a little creativity and these simple steps, you can bring the excitement of cosmic bowling right into your living room. Turn up the music, grab your glow-in-the-dark gear, and get ready for a night of strikes, laughter, and unforgettable memories.

Activity 72: Family Dance Party

Turn up the energy and groove to the beat with a Family Dance Party! This exhilarating activity brings a burst of fun, laughter, and fitness to your living room, all while bonding with your loved ones.

Materials Needed:

- A playlist of upbeat songs
- A clear space in your living room or any suitable area

Step-by-Step Instructions:

1. Set the Mood: Choose a variety of songs that are upbeat and suitable for dancing. Create a playlist that everyone can enjoy, including songs from different genres.
2. Clear the Space: Move furniture or any obstacles to create a safe and open dance floor. Make sure there's enough room for everyone to move freely.
3. Create a Playlist: Use your favorite music streaming platform to create a playlist of songs that make you want to move. Consider including a mix of old and new tunes to cater to different tastes.
4. Dance Styles: Spice things up by incorporating different dance styles into your dance party. You can try Zumba routines, Latin dance moves, hip-hop steps, or even freestyle dancing.
5. Invite Everyone: Gather your family members and let them know it's time for a dance party! Encourage everyone to join in, regardless of their dance experience.
6. Switch Styles: After a few songs, switch to a different dance style. This keeps the energy high and adds variety to the experience.
7. Encourage Participation: If you have family members who might be hesitant to dance, create an inclusive and supportive environment. Emphasize that it's all about having fun and being active.
8. Cool Down: Slow down the tempo and conclude the dance party with a cool-down. Stretch your muscles gently to prevent any post-dance soreness.

Benefits:

- Cardiovascular Workout: Dancing is a fantastic aerobic exercise that boosts heart health and burns calories.
- Coordination and Balance: Dancing improves coordination and balance, enhancing physical skills.

The Family Dance Party is a lively and enjoyable way to stay active while spending quality time together. Let the music guide you as you dance your way to a healthier and happier family.

Activity 73: Family Hiking Adventure

Embark on an invigorating journey with your loved ones through the beauty of nature with a Family Hiking Adventure. Hiking not only offers a fantastic workout but also creates lasting memories and connections.

Materials Needed:
- Comfortable hiking shoes
- Appropriate clothing for the weather
- Backpack with essentials (water, snacks, first aid kit, sunscreen)
- Trail map or GPS device

Step-by-Step Instructions:
1. Choose a Trail: Research hiking trails in your area that are suitable for your family's fitness level and experience. Look for trails with varying difficulty levels and scenic views.
2. Plan Ahead: Check the trail length, elevation gain, and estimated time to complete the hike. Ensure the trail aligns with your family's capabilities.
3. Pack Essentials: Load your backpack with water bottles to stay hydrated, energy-boosting snacks, a basic first aid kit, and sunscreen. Dress in layers to adjust to changing weather conditions.
4. Safety First: Inform someone about your hiking plans and expected return time. Carry a fully charged mobile phone and a trail map or GPS device.
5. Start Early: Begin your hike early in the day to avoid midday heat and crowds. Set a pace that is comfortable for the entire family, taking breaks when needed.
6. Enjoy the Views: Take in the beauty of the outdoors as you hike. Encourage your family to stop and appreciate the scenic spots along the way.
7. Complete the Scavenger Hunt (Optional): If you've created a scavenger hunt, work together to find the items on your checklist. It adds an element of adventure and fun to the hike.
8. Capture Memories: Bring a camera to capture the breathtaking views and precious moments. These photos will serve as cherished mementos of your family's hiking adventure.

Benefits:
- Nature Connection: Hiking allows your family to disconnect from screens and immerse in the natural world.
- Physical Activity: Hiking provides an excellent cardiovascular workout and helps build endurance.

As you lace up your hiking boots and venture onto the trail, you're creating memories, building bonds, and discovering the wonders of the world together as a family.

Activity 74: Family Yoga Session

Indulge in a serene and rejuvenating experience with your family through a Family Yoga Session. This harmonious activity not only fosters physical well-being but also cultivates mindfulness and strengthens the family's connection.

Materials Needed:

- Comfortable clothing suitable for movement
- Yoga mats or soft surface
- Calming music (optional)
- Open minds and positive energy

Step-by-Step Instructions:

1. Choose a Quiet Space: Find a peaceful and clutter-free area in your home or a tranquil spot outdoors where your family can practice yoga without distractions.
2. Set the Mood: Dim the lights and play soft, soothing music to create a serene ambiance for the yoga session.
3. Basic Poses: If your family is new to yoga, start with basic poses, such as Child's Pose, Downward Dog, Cat-Cow, and Mountain Pose.
4. Breathing Awareness: Guide your family in mindful breathing. Inhale deeply through the nose, feeling the breath expand the belly, and exhale slowly through the mouth, releasing tension.
5. Progressive Poses: Gradually introduce more challenging poses as your family gains confidence and flexibility.
6. Partner Poses (Optional): For added fun and connection, try partner yoga poses. Poses like Double Downward Dog or Seated Forward Fold with a partner can deepen the bond among family members.
7. Guided Meditation: After the yoga sequence, guide your family through a brief meditation. Encourage them to focus on their breath, release stress, and find mental clarity.

Benefits:

- Physical Fitness: Yoga promotes flexibility, balance, and strength while being gentle on the body.
- Stress Relief: Mindful movements and deep breathing reduce stress and anxiety.

Through Family Yoga Sessions, you create an oasis of tranquility and unity amidst the busyness of life. As you breathe, stretch, and move together, you're nurturing your family's physical and emotional well-being while forging a deeper bond that radiates harmony.

Activity 75: Family Water Sports Adventure

Dive into the refreshing world of water sports and create unforgettable memories with your family. From the gentle embrace of kayaking to the exhilaration of paddleboarding, water activities offer a fantastic way to stay active and enjoy the great outdoors.

Materials Needed:

- Appropriate swimwear
- Life jackets for safety
- Water sports equipment (kayaks, paddleboards, surfboards)
- Sunscreen and hats
- Water-resistant bags for valuables

- Refreshments and water bottles

Step-by-Step Instructions:

1. Select the Water Activity: Choose a water sport that suits your family's interests and fitness levels. Whether it's swimming, kayaking, paddleboarding, or a combination of activities, ensure everyone is comfortable with the chosen option.

2. Safety First: Before you embark on your water adventure, familiarize yourself with safety guidelines. Make sure everyone wears properly fitting life jackets and is aware of any specific rules or regulations for the chosen water activity.

3. Choose a Location: Find a suitable water body, such as a calm lake, river, or even the ocean if you're experienced and comfortable.

4. Warm-Up and Stretch: Start with a light warm-up to prepare your muscles for the activity. Gently stretch to prevent injuries and promote flexibility.

5. Introduction and Instruction: If trying a new water sport, provide a brief introduction and basic instructions to the family. Cover techniques for staying balanced, paddling, and navigating.

6. Beginner-Friendly: Keep the pace beginner-friendly, especially if some family members are new to the chosen water sport.

7. Explore and Play: Once everyone feels confident, explore the water body together. Engage in playful activities, such as friendly races, team challenges, or simply enjoying the serenity of being on the water.

Benefits:

- Family Bonding: Sharing an outdoor adventure fosters unity and strengthens family bonds.
- Skill Building: Learning a new water sport enhances coordination and self-confidence.

By engaging in water sports as a family, you're embracing the joy of movement while immersing yourselves in the beauty of nature. The gentle waves become a playground of shared laughter and discovery, making every splash a cherished memory.

Activity 76: Family Cycling Adventure

Embrace the thrill of the open road and embark on a family cycling adventure. Biking not only offers a fantastic cardiovascular workout but also presents the perfect opportunity to explore your surroundings and share quality time with your loved ones.

Materials Needed:

- Bicycles for each family member
- Helmets and protective gear
- Comfortable attire and sneakers
- Water bottles and hydration packs
- Maps or GPS devices for navigation
- Bike trailer or child seat for younger riders

Step-by-Step Instructions:

1. Gear Up: Ensure everyone has well-fitted helmets and appropriate attire. Adjust the bikes to match each family member's height and comfort.

2. Choose Your Route: Decide whether you want to explore local trails and bike paths – or venture out for a longer ride. Research scenic routes that cater to your family's skill level.

3. Safety Briefing: Before setting off, review basic bike safety rules. Teach hand signals for turns and remind everyone to stay on designated paths.

4. Warm-Up: Begin with a gentle warm-up to get your muscles ready for the ride. Start with slower pedaling and gradually increase your pace.

5. Mindful Riding: Encourage everyone to ride at a comfortable pace and be mindful of their surroundings. Use the ride as an opportunity to relax and clear your mind.

6. Family Games: Add an element of fun by incorporating family-friendly biking games. Challenge each other to a friendly race or create a scavenger hunt based on items you might encounter during the ride.

7. Rest Stops: Plan rest stops along the route. Use these breaks to stretch, enjoy a snack, and rest before continuing your journey.

Benefits:

- Cardiovascular Workout: Biking provides an excellent cardiovascular exercise that's gentle on the joints.

- Mental Refreshment: Biking in nature offers a mental break from daily routines.

As you pedal together, the wind in your hair becomes a shared sense of freedom, and each mile covered is a testament to your family's unity and determination. Whether you're cycling through urban trails or countryside lanes, the journey itself becomes a cherished memory etched in the pavement.

Activity 77: Family Sports Tournament

Ignite the spirit of healthy competition within your family by organizing a thrilling sports tournament. Whether it's football, basketball, volleyball, or any other sport, a family sports tournament is an exhilarating way to bond, showcase your skills, and create lasting memories.

Materials Needed:

- Sports equipment based on the chosen sport (soccer ball, basketball, volleyball)
- Court or playing area suitable for the sport
- Team jerseys or colored bands to distinguish teams
- Water bottles and hydration stations
- First aid kit for any minor injuries

Step-by-Step Instructions:

1. Choose the Sport: Discuss with your family and select a sport that everyone enjoys and can participate in comfortably. Consider the space available and any safety concerns.

2. Form Teams: Divide the family into teams. To promote camaraderie, mix different ages and skill levels within each team.

3. Set the Rules: Establish clear and age-appropriate rules for the chosen sport. Make sure everyone understands the rules and expectations.

4. Prepare the Venue: Set up the playing area according to the sport's requirements. For example, mark boundaries on a field, set up a basketball hoop, or create a volleyball court.

5. Warm-Up: Begin with a group warm-up to prevent injuries. Incorporate dynamic stretches and light cardio to prepare the muscles for physical activity.

6. Friendly Matches: Organize a series of matches between the teams. Keep the matches light-hearted and fun, emphasizing the spirit of friendly competition.

7. Cheering Squad: Designate some family members as the cheering squad for each team. Encourage positive cheering and sportsmanship.

8. Hydration Breaks: Schedule regular breaks for water and rest. Staying hydrated is essential, especially during physical activities.

9. Team Bonding: Between matches, provide opportunities for teams to strategize, bond, and discuss their game plan.

10. Tournament Finale: After all matches are completed, celebrate with a friendly awards ceremony. Recognize teamwork, sportsmanship, and any outstanding performances.

Benefits:

- Healthy Competition: A sports tournament fosters friendly competition and encourages everyone to give their best.
- Teamwork: Working together in teams promotes collaboration and communication.

As you dive into the heart-pounding matches, every pass, shot, and goal becomes a shared triumph. The laughter, cheers, and even the occasional playful rivalry create a tapestry of memories that will stay with your family long after the tournament ends.

Activity 78: Family Olympics

Bring the spirit of friendly competition and sportsmanship to your family with a mini Olympics. This multi-sport event allows everyone to participate in various challenges and games, fostering teamwork and active fun.

Materials Needed:

- Sports equipment, such as balls, cones, hula hoops, jump ropes, etc.
- Stopwatch or timer
- Prizes or ribbons for winners (optional)

Step-by-Step Instructions:

1. Select Activities: Choose a variety of activities that family members can compete in. These can include relay races, sack races, hula hoop contests, soccer dribbling, and more.

2. Set Up Stations: Arrange different stations for each activity. Ensure there's enough space for each challenge.

3. Demonstrate Activities: Briefly explain each activity and demonstrate how it's done. Make sure everyone understands the rules and objectives.

4. Team Assignments: Divide the family into teams or pairs. Mix up the teams to encourage bonding and collaboration.

5. Rotate and Compete: Assign a specific time for each station. Family members rotate through the stations, competing in the activities and trying to earn points for their team.

6. Tally Points: Keep track of points earned by each team throughout the mini Olympics.

7. Celebrate and Award: At the end of all the activities, gather everyone and announce the winning team. You can award prizes or ribbons to celebrate their achievements.

Benefits:

- Healthy Competition: Friendly competition promotes teamwork, sportsmanship, and a healthy spirit of rivalry.

- Positive Memories: The shared experience of competing and celebrating fosters cherished memories.

As the family engages in a range of athletic challenges, the cheers, laughter, and determination remind everyone that being part of a team, regardless of who wins, is the true victory.

Activity 79: Frizbee Fenzie

Step into the world of outdoor fun with a thrilling game of Frizbee Fenzie. It's an energetic combination of Ultimate Frisbee and tag that guarantees laughter, teamwork, and active enjoyment for the entire family.

Materials Needed:

- Frisbee (multiple if possible)
- Open outdoor spaces like a park or a field
- Cones or markers to designate boundaries

Step-by-Step Instructions:

1. Set the Boundaries: Choose an open outdoor area and mark the boundaries using cones or other markers.

2. Form Teams: Divide your family into two teams. You can assign teams randomly or mix up the ages and abilities for more balance.

3. Understand the Rules: Explain the rules of the game to your family. Frizbee Fenzie is a combination of tag and Ultimate Frisbee, where players aim to catch the frisbee while avoiding being tagged.

4. Start the Game: Begin the game by having one team throw the frisbee to the other team. The receiving team must catch the frisbee to gain control.

5. Pass and Score: The team in control of the frisbee works together to pass it among themselves. The goal is to successfully pass the frisbee to a teammate in the opponent's end zone, scoring a point.

6. Avoid Being Tagged: The other team aims to tag the player with the frisbee. Once tagged, that player must stop moving and pivot on one foot. They can still pass the frisbee to teammates but cannot move.

7. Tagged Players Rejoin: If a tagged player receives a pass from a teammate, they are freed from

being tagged and can move again.

8. Interception and Turnover: If a frisbee is not caught by the receiving team or is intercepted by the opposing team, possession changes, and the game continues.

9. Scoring and Winning: Keep track of points for each successful pass leading to a score. The team with the most points at the end of the game wins.

Benefits:

- Strategy and Coordination: Players develop strategies for passing and catching while coordinating their movements.
- Fun and Laughter: The blend of Ultimate Frisbee and tag guarantees laughter and enjoyment for the whole family.

Frizbee Fenzie brings a dash of excitement and an abundance of fun to your family outdoor time. As frisbees soar through the air and players dash around, bonds strengthen, and shared memories are woven into the fabric of your family's journey. So, gear up and unleash the frisbee frenzy!

Activity 80: The Water Balloon Challenge

Get ready to make a splash with the thrilling and refreshing family water balloon challenge. This exhilarating relay game will have your family working together, laughing, and cooling off in the best way possible.

Materials Needed:

- Water balloons (prepare a generous supply)
- Buckets or containers filled with water
- Open outdoor spaces like a yard or park
- Towels and swim gear (because things might get wet!)

Step-by-Step Instructions:

1. Set Up the Game Area: Choose a spacious outdoor area for the water balloon challenge. Lay out the buckets of water and place them at a comfortable distance from each other.

2. Form Teams: Divide your family into teams. You can have two or more teams, depending on the number of participants.

3. Create a Relay Line: Each team lines up behind their designated bucket of water. Make sure there's ample space between the teams to avoid collisions.

4. Fill the Balloons: Have each team member fill a water balloon from their team's bucket. Make sure the balloons are filled to a size that's easy to handle and won't burst too easily.

5. Ready, Set, Go!: Start the challenge by having the first players from each team hold their water balloons. When the game begins, they race towards a designated point and back while carrying the water balloon.

6. Pass the Balloon: Upon returning to their team, the first players pass the water balloon to the second players. The second player then repeats the process, racing with the balloon to the designated point and back.

7. Keep Passing and Racing: The relay continues with each team member taking a turn. As the water balloons are passed and raced with, some might burst, adding an extra element of surprise

and excitement.

8. Finish Line and Victory: The relay ends when all team members have completed their turns. The first team to have all members finish the relay wins the water balloon challenge.

Benefits:

- Reflexes and Coordination: Players improve their reflexes and hand-eye coordination as they handle and pass water balloons.

- Outdoor Fun: The game encourages outdoor play and enjoying the sun while staying cool.

The water balloon challenge is a fantastic way to create joyful memories and beat the heat during the summer months. As water balloons soar through the air and laughter fills the atmosphere, the bonds between family members grow stronger. So, put on your swim gear, grab those water balloons, and dive into a world of watery excitement with your loved ones!

Families that play together stay together! Regarding bonding experiences, few things can beat getting active as a family. Whether going for a bike ride, having a picnic in the park, or even a friendly game of soccer, family activities for fitness and fun are a great way to strengthen the bond between family members and promote healthy lifestyles. But why stop at just your own family? Involving other families in these activities expands your social circle and creates opportunities for new friendships and shared memories. So, gather your family and friends, and get ready to have fun while staying fit!

Chapter 9: Traveling Together: Day Trip Ideas

There's nothing quite like going on a day trip with people you love. Traveling together is a beautiful way to create lasting memories and strengthen relationships. When it comes to day trips, the options are endless. You could spend the day exploring a nearby city, hiking through a nearby park, or hitting an amusement park. The best part is that you don't need to plan and book an entire vacation.

Benefits of Shared Family Adventures

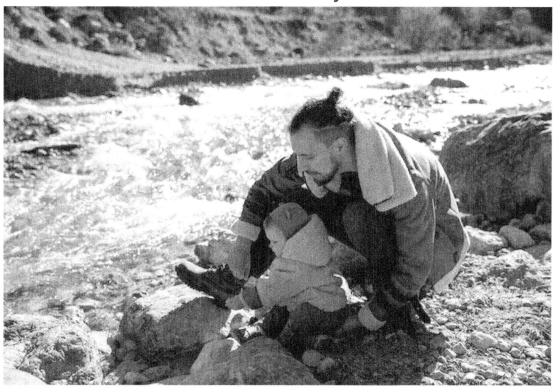

Day trips with family can strengthen your bond.
https://www.pexels.com/photo/father-with-little-kid-resting-on-rocky-ground-near-river-in-mountains-3933498/

Spending quality time with family members is essential to a happy and healthy family life. But in our fast-paced world, where everyone juggles work, school, and other commitments, family time often takes a backseat. However, taking on a shared family adventure is a perfect way to bond, create lasting memories, and even learn new things together.

- **Strengthened Bond**: Shared family adventures help create a stronger bond between family members. Participating in an activity together creates an opportunity to create happy memories. Whether it's a hiking trip, trying new foods, or teaming up for a sport, families must work together to overcome challenges, learn new things, and share a joyful experience. These shared experiences make family members feel closer, strengthening the family bond.

- **Educational Value:** Shared family adventures offer a learning opportunity for everyone involved. There's always something new to discover, whether it's learning about nature, history, or different cultures. Families can visit museums and historical sites, take guided tours, or even study a new language together. Learning together helps engender interest, curiosity, and an appreciation for other cultures and ways of life.

- **Cultural Exploration:** Shared family adventures allow for the exploration of different cultures, foods, and traditions. Families who travel to new places can experience the unique customs and practices of people from other regions and countries. For instance, trying traditional dishes, visiting local markets, and attending cultural festivals can expose you and your family to new perspectives and help develop a better understanding of different cultures.

- **Recreational Activities:** Shared family adventures offer a chance to participate in recreational activities like swimming, surfing, hiking, camping, and biking, among others. These activities help promote an active lifestyle, boost physical health, and enhance mental well-being. Participating in outdoor activities also allows family members to unplug from technology and connect with nature, which can be therapeutic.

Simple Trip Ideas and Their Benefits

Are you looking for an affordable family trip close to home that doesn't require much planning? Plenty of simple trip ideas for families can boost your family's happiness, strengthen your relationships, and create special memories without breaking the bank. Here are three trip ideas your whole family will love!

Activity 81: Shopping Outlets

Who doesn't love a shopping trip? Shopping outlets are a go-to for families looking for a fun and exciting outing. It is a great way to spend quality time together, and shopping outlets are often located in scenic areas where you can take a walk and enjoy the local scenery and landscape. As you walk around, you will find items to add to your cart, then enjoy the thought of bagging discounts galore! You can also pack a picnic lunch and enjoy some outdoor fun at a nearby park or take in the local attractions.

Activity 82: Local Zoo/Aquarium

A visit to the zoo or aquarium is always a great trip idea for families. It's both educational and entertaining, and you and your kids will learn new things about the animals and their habitats. A visit to the zoo or aquarium can also allow your child to learn more about conservation and environmental issues. Encourage your child to ask plenty of questions to learn more about the animals they meet. Plus, there is nothing like watching animals in their natural habitats or learning about the under-the-sea creatures that make you appreciate the world beyond your backyard.

Activity 83: Museum Outing

Museum outings are a fantastic way to introduce your children to art, history, and other cultures. Even young children can develop and appreciate their creativity and imagination through museum exhibits. Exposure to different art forms and cultural experiences can encourage children to think outside the box and expand their perspectives. Some museums even offer special events for kids, such as scavenger hunts to engage the younger minds. Why not take your family to discover some of the world's most fascinating exhibitions?

Activity 84: Bike Ride

If the weather is nice, why not take your family on a bike ride? It's an easy way to get everyone outdoors and active while having fun. Plus, it's a great way to explore new places together and share stories along the ride. With some simple research, you will be able to find trails for all levels of cyclists in your area. Bring snacks and plenty of water to keep everyone energized!

Activity 85: Beach Trip

Nothing beats a beach trip for a day of fun in the sun. Pack up some outdoor games, sunscreen, and your beach bag with towels and sandwiches for a perfect day out! The beach is also a great place to practice activities, such as swimming, surfing, and kayaking. And, of course, the beach is a great place to relax and enjoy quality family time.

Activity 86: Local Nature Trails

Hiking with your family is the perfect way to appreciate nature at its best. Find a peaceful spot in your area and get out there to explore the natural wonders of your local environment. It's also an excellent opportunity to engage kids in conversations about wildlife, plants, and trees. Bring along some binoculars for a closer look at the flora and fauna!

Activity 87: Outdoor Movie Night

Enjoy a unique movie night experience with your family by setting up an outdoor theatre. All you need is some popcorn, comfortable seating and blankets to snuggle up in, and a projector or laptop to show the movie of your choice. To make it extra special, set up some lawn chairs around the screen for a more classic cinema feel. For added fun, you could even turn the movie night into a real outdoor movie party and invite friends, family, and neighbors to join in!

Activity 88: Amusement Park

What better way to enjoy the summer than at an amusement park? There are plenty of fun activities for all ages, including roller coasters, bumper cars, and water rides, perfect for a day full of thrills and laughter. Or, if you're looking for something more relaxed, some parks offer mini golfing, Ferris wheels, and carousels for a more laid-back experience. Make sure to pack comfortable clothes and shoes for the day's activities!

Activity 89: Water Park

Beat the summer heat with a trip to the nearest water park! You can plunge into exciting attractions, such as inner tubes, body slides, lazy rivers, wave pools, and so much more. The little ones can even enjoy some of the kiddie slides and pools. There is something for everyone to enjoy! Pack swimsuits, towels, and sunscreen for a fantastic day out in the water.

Activity 90: National Parks

Explore the wonders of nature with your family at a national park. Hiking trails, swimming holes, geysers, canyons, and stunning views are just some of the attractions you can find in national parks. Take your time to appreciate the beauty of nature while learning more about the environment and its creatures. Bring along a camera for some everlasting memories!

Activity 91: Trampoline Park

Bounce off those energy levels with a trip to a trampoline park! With wall-to-wall trampolines, foam pits, and lots of other fun activities, such as dodgeball and basketball, the whole family is sure to have an amazing time. Make sure everyone's wearing comfortable clothing that won't restrict their movements for this fun activity.

Activity 92: Outdoor Concert

Enjoy a night of music and entertainment with your family at an outdoor concert. You can find all sorts of events, such as jazz and blues, country, rock, and more. Choose something for everyone in the family to enjoy! Pack some snacks and comfortable seating to relax while listening to great music under the stars.

Activity 93: Mini Golf

Get out on the golf course with your family and have a friendly competition! Mini golf is great for all ages, from young kids to adults. It's also an excellent way to practice teamwork and sportsmanship while having fun together. Plus, some mini golf courses offer additional activities, such as go-karts or batting cages, for the whole family to enjoy.

Activity 94: Kayaking

Learn the basics of kayaking with your family and explore the waters around you. It's a great way to get out and enjoy quality time together while getting some exercise. Wear life vests, bring plenty of water and snacks, and practice safety guidelines for a fun but safe day out on the water. It's sure to be an adventure you won't forget!

Activity 95: Ziplining

Take your family on an exciting adventure with a zipline tour! You'll be soaring high above the treetops and enjoying spectacular forest views. Wear comfortable clothes, closed-toe shoes, and safety gear for this thrilling activity. It's a great way to get the adrenaline pumping and create lasting memories for everyone.

Activity 96: Rock Climbing

Challenge yourself and your family to a rock climbing adventure! This is a great way to bond, build trust, and have fun while getting some exercise at the same time. If you're new to the activity, there are plenty of indoor rock climbing gyms that offer classes and rentals for beginners. Wear comfortable clothes and appropriate shoes for the activity.

Activity 97: Outdoor Yoga

Get your body moving with some outdoor yoga! All you need is a yoga mat, a peaceful spot outdoors, and your family for a great way to relax while stretching out those muscles. Plus, there are plenty of online classes available if you don't have a yoga instructor handy.

Activity 98: Flashlight Tag

Take the game of tag to the next level with flashlights! Play it indoors or outdoors after dark, adding an element of stealth and excitement. You can even incorporate different challenges like finding hidden clues or completing tasks to add another layer of fun.

Activity 99: Fishing

Spend a day out fishing with the whole family! You can find plenty of lakes, rivers, and streams where you can fish for some of your favorite species, such as trout, bass, catfish, or panfish. Bring the right gear, such as rods, reels, bait, and other necessary equipment for a successful day out on the water.

Activity 100: Nature Walks

Get some fresh air and explore nature with your family on a nature walk. Bring binoculars to spot some birds or look for tracks in the mud. Talk about different plants and trees you find along the way, or take pictures of anything that catches your eye. It's a great way to enjoy the great outdoors and have some quality time together!

Whether your family loves shopping, being outdoors, or learning about history or wildlife, these simple trip ideas can provide endless opportunities for bonding, learning, and exploring together. In addition, they are easy to plan, budget-friendly, and convenient to get out of the house and experience something new.

Day trip planning can be both exciting and overwhelming. But with these practical tips, you can be sure you will make the most of your next-day trip. Remember that travel is about making memories and experiencing new things, so don't let the planning process weigh you down. Instead, stay flexible, prioritize your itinerary, and enjoy the journey as much as the destination. Bon Voyage!

Chapter 10: Celebrating Togetherness: Family Traditions to Cherish

Family traditions are the backbone of togetherness. Celebrating these moments with our loved ones creates a bond that transcends time and distance. Whether gathering around the table for a special meal, coming together for a holiday, or just enjoying a Sunday evening ritual, these traditions make our families unique. They are the threads that weave our individual stories into one cohesive narrative. Whenever we look back on these cherished memories, we are reminded of the love and laughter we shared with those we hold dear.

Family traditions create bonds that last through generations.
https://www.pexels.com/photo/family-sitting-at-table-3807395/

Ultimately, there is something magical about celebrating togetherness and family traditions. They help us connect in profound, meaningful, and unforgettable ways. This chapter explores the importance of family traditions, provides some ideas for customizing celebrations, and offers tips on establishing and maintaining these rituals over time. By the end of this chapter, readers will understand why family traditions matter and be inspired to create meaningful connections.

Exploring the Benefits of Family Traditions

Family traditions have the power to connect us to our heritage, deepen ties, and create lasting memories that shape our lives. Whether it's a celebratory meal, story or games night, or an annual family vacation, these traditions provide a sense of stability and meaning that can support us through life's challenges. By honoring our traditions, we pass down values and beliefs from generation to generation, preserving our cultural identity and reinforcing the importance of community. The beauty of our traditions is that they hold the key to a more prosperous, more fulfilling existence.

Cultivating a Sense of Belonging through Shared Customs

Belonging is a fundamental human need. And nothing makes us feel more connected than shared customs. Whether it's a special ceremony, a yearly tradition, or a daily routine, customs provide comfort, familiarity, and community. They bond us like a family and make us feel part of something bigger than ourselves. By cultivating a sense of belonging through shared customs, we create an environment where everyone feels valued, respected, and supported. Customs shape our identity, define our culture and heritage, and remind us of our roots. They unify us in times of joy and sorrow and create lifetime memories.

Ideas for Celebrating Special Occasions

When celebrating special occasions with family, the possibilities are endless. But if you're looking for fresh ideas to create lasting memories, consider starting a weekly or monthly gratitude jar. This simple yet powerful tradition involves taking a few moments each week or month to reflect on what you're thankful for and writing it down on paper, which is then added to a jar. Then, at the end of the year, you can revisit everything you were grateful for as a family.

An annual family photo shoot is another great way to celebrate special occasions. It gives you a beautiful keepsake to cherish for years to come and an opportunity to get everyone together and create new memories. And, of course, no celebration is complete without food! Consider designating one night each month for a special celebratory dinner, where you can cook a special meal together, dress up, and enjoy each other's company. With these ideas, you will create memorable occasions that your family will treasure for years.

Activity 101: Create and Preserve Family Traditions

Family traditions are the threads that weave the fabric of a close-knit family. They create lasting memories, strengthen bonds, and instill a sense of belonging. If you're looking to establish and maintain meaningful family traditions, follow these steps.

Materials Needed:

- Pen and paper or digital device for note-taking
- A family calendar

Step-by-Step Instructions:

1. Reflect on Values and Interests: Gather your family and engage in a thoughtful discussion about your shared values and interests. What activities or rituals hold significance to all family members?

2. Brainstorm Ideas: Encourage each family member to brainstorm ideas for potential traditions. Consider various occasions, such as weekly routines, holidays, birthdays, or annual vacations.

3. Set a Schedule: Decide on the frequency and timing of your traditions. Will they be daily, weekly, monthly, or annually? Create a family calendar to track them.

4. Choose Activities: Select specific activities or rituals that align with your family's values and interests. These could range from game nights and movie nights to hiking trips or volunteering together.

5. Involve Everyone: Ensure that all family members have a say in the traditions you establish. Their involvement will foster a sense of ownership and enthusiasm.

6. Document Your Traditions: Create a document or journal that outlines the details of each tradition. Include the purpose, activities involved, and any special instructions.

7. Implement and Adapt: Begin implementing your chosen traditions and stick to your schedule. Be open to adaptations or improvements as you gain experience.

8. Pass It On: Encourage the passing down of traditions from one generation to the next. This ensures the continuity and preservation of your family's legacy.

Benefits:

- Cherished Memories: Traditions lead to cherished memories that can be revisited and shared over the years.

- Legacy Building: Traditions become part of your family's legacy, connecting generations.

Remember that family traditions should be flexible and adaptable to changing circumstances. They should evolve as your family grows and matures. By establishing and maintaining traditions that reflect your family's uniqueness, you'll create a strong bond that will endure through the generations. So, gather your family and start building traditions that will be cherished for a lifetime.

There's something extraordinary about the power of family traditions. From passing down secret recipes and putting up holiday decorations to taking annual vacations and attending milestone events, these rituals create a bond that transcends time and distance. They allow us to connect with our loved ones in a way that feels both familiar and profound. And what's even more incredible is that the power of family traditions extends far beyond our immediate family members. When we share these customs with our communities and cultural groups, we strengthen our bonds. It's beautiful to be part of something bigger than ourselves. Family traditions provide us with that sense of connection. So, honor these unique customs and embrace their power to bring us closer together.

Conclusion

Spending quality time together is vital to building strong bonds and creating lasting memories as a family. You can do countless indoor or outdoor activities together, regardless of your interests or age. There's something for everyone, from hiking and camping to board games and movie nights. You can even turn mundane tasks like cooking or cleaning into fun family bonding time by involving everyone and turning it into a friendly competition. The possibilities are endless, and the benefits are priceless. You will create beautiful memories and strengthen your relationships, improve communication, and learn new things about each other.

In today's digital age, it's easy to lose sight of the importance of bonding with our loved ones. Screens have become our primary source of entertainment, but they seldom provide the meaningful experiences we need to forge strong connections. That's why now, it's more crucial than ever to find screen-free activities and outdoor adventures to unite families.

This guide covered some of the best ways to spend quality time with your family indoors, outdoors, and even on day trips. Whether hiking through the mountains, playing board games, or simply spending time in nature, these experiences create lasting memories that you and your loved ones will treasure for years to come. By building these bonds, we strengthen our relationships and develop a foundation of trust that can withstand the trials of daily life.

Traveling with family is an incredible opportunity to create unforgettable memories and strengthen the ties of togetherness. This guide also provided some day trip ideas that allow you to explore the world around you and create incredible memories with your loved ones. From hikes to camping trips, day trips are an excellent way to explore new destinations, immerse yourselves in different cultures, and share fascinating experiences. The possibilities are endless, whether it's a scenic drive along the coast, visiting a historical site, or hiking up a mountain trail.

However, the journey itself is just as important as the destination. To enhance the experience, consider creating family traditions you can cherish for years. It could be a song you sing together, a game you play in the car, or a particular food you always eat on the way. Whatever it is, these little yet meaningful traditions can bring you closer and make your travels more memorable. So, pack your bags, hit the road, and celebrate the joy of togetherness with your loved ones.

Part 2: Positive Behavior Activities for Kids

101 Fun Games and Exercises for Cultivating Kindness, Social Skills, and Good Habits

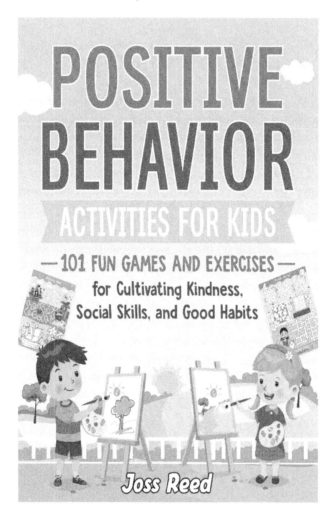

Introduction

In a constantly changing and evolving world, it is essential to equip our children with the tools they need to navigate life with kindness, empathy, and positive behavior.

As parents, caregivers, and educators, we have a unique opportunity to shape the future by fostering a positive environment that encourages children's development of essential social skills and good habits. This book is designed to be your go-to resource, filled with engaging activities and games to make learning about kindness and positive behavior enjoyable for kids of all ages.

The journey towards cultivating kindness and positive behavior begins with understanding their significance. By instilling these values in our children, we empower them to create a positive impact on their surroundings. Kindness is not only about being polite and considerate; it is a mindset that promotes inclusivity, compassion, and respect for oneself and others.

The activities in this book are carefully crafted to foster the development of various social skills and good habits, empowering children to build strong relationships, make responsible choices, and thrive in various social settings. From teamwork and communication to problem-solving and emotional intelligence, each activity is designed to make learning fun, interactive, and relatable.

With 101 different games and exercises, you'll find various activities catering to different age groups, interests, and learning styles. Whether you're a parent looking to enhance your child's character development at home, a teacher searching for engaging classroom activities, or a caregiver hoping to create a positive and nurturing environment, this book supports you at every step.

Remember, creating a positive impact on a child's behavior is collaborative. This book serves as a starting point, providing you with a toolkit to inspire and guide the children in your life. It's a call to action to invest in our children's future by prioritizing the development of their character, emotional intelligence, and social skills.

Chapter 1: Kick Off with Kindness

"Three things in human life are important: the first is to be kind; the second is to be kind; and the third is to be kind." - Henry James.

As a parent or caregiver, you hold the key to nurturing kindness in your child, an essential element of their development and overall well-being. According to prominent social psychologist Martin L. Hoffman, children exhibit signs of empathy in their infancy, suggesting that these emotions are innate and develop as early as the first year of life (Hoffman, 2000). By providing your child opportunities to practice kindness, you foster their empathetic instincts and support their growth into compassionate individuals.

In addition to building empathy, promoting kindness has numerous benefits, as emphasized by several psychological theories. For instance, the Attachment Theory, proposed by British psychologist John Bowlby, highlights the significance of forming strong emotional bonds between children and their caregivers (Bowlby, 1973). Acts of kindness can help strengthen these emotional ties, leading to a sense of security and, ultimately, a healthier emotional development.

Moreover, Social Cognitive Theory, founded by psychologist Albert Bandura, posits that people, particularly children, learn through observation and imitation (Bandura, 1977). When you model kindness for your child, you create an environment that encourages them to replicate these actions – a demonstration of Bandura's observations. This is also why it's crucial for you, as a parent or caregiver, to exemplify kindness in your everyday life, as your child's social behavior is shaped through observing the world around them.

Furthermore, positive parenting techniques based on concepts such as Diana Baumrind's "authoritative parenting style" emphasize the importance of warmth, emotional support, and behavioral guidance (Baumrind, 1967). By actively encouraging and facilitating kindness in your child's life, you employ the core principles of authoritative parenting – fostering emotional well-being, independence, social competence, and resilience.

In conclusion, various psychology-based theories highlight the significance of fostering kindness in children – helping them build healthy relationships, develop emotional intelligence, and acquire social skills. By providing a nurturing environment and involving your child in kindness-promoting activities, you contribute significantly to their overall development and well-being.

Benefits of Kindness in Children's Development

Teaching kindness to children has many benefits that promote overall well-being and contribute to their lifelong success. One significant advantage is the boost in self-esteem kids develop as they engage in acts of kindness, which helps them feel more confident and capable in various aspects of their lives.

Social and emotional growth is another essential aspect of children's development enhanced by kindness. Through activities promoting empathy and compassion, kids learn to form meaningful connections with those around them, fostering strong friendships and support networks throughout life.

These positive values also impact academic performance; studies show that students who display kindness and respect are likelier to excel in school due to improved attention spans and creative thinking abilities.

Activities

Activity 1: Kindness Jar

Create a Kindness Jar where kids can write down their acts of kindness on small pieces of paper and place them in the jar. Encourage them to fill up the jar over time and read the notes together as a family at the end of each month.

Instructions:

1. Find a jar and decorate it with stickers, ribbons, or paint.
2. Place the jar in a central location in the home.
3. Provide small, colorful pieces of paper and a pen.
4. Encourage the kids to write down their acts of kindness on the paper and place them in the jar.
5. At the end of each month, gather as a family and read the kindness notes together.

Activity 2: Compliment Cards

Kids will create compliment cards for their friends, family members, or teachers to express appreciation and encouragement.

Instructions:

1. Print the provided compliment card template.
2. Have the kids cut out the cards.
3. Encourage the kids to write kind compliments or words of encouragement on each card.
4. Ask the kids to give the compliment cards to others as a surprise act of kindness.

To:_____

From:_____

_____

_____

To:_____

From:_____

_____

_____

To:_____

From:_____

_____

_____

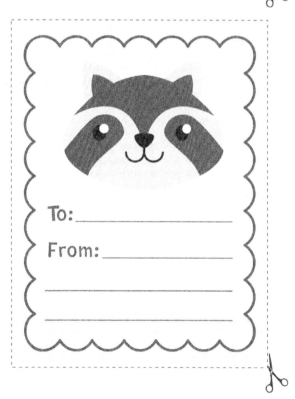

To:_____

From:_____

_____

_____

Activity 3: The Daisy Chain of Kindness

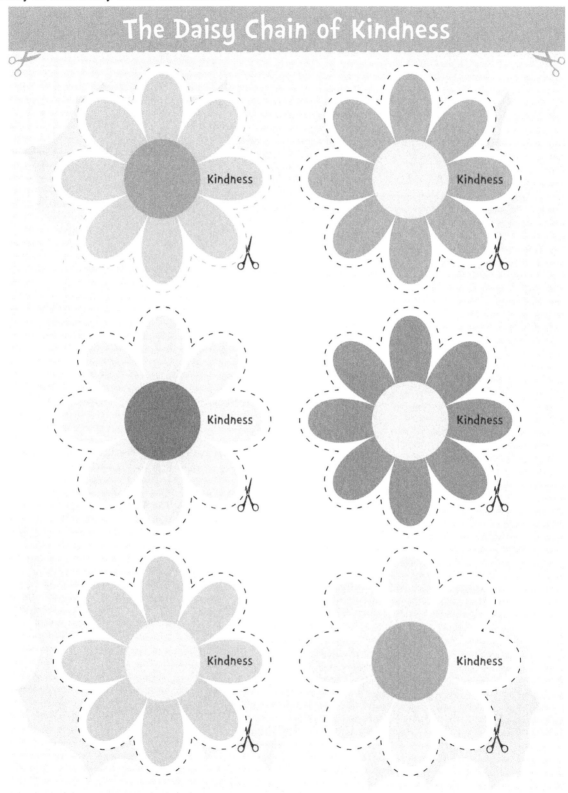

The Daisy Chain of Kindness

Kindness

Kindness

Kindness

Kindness

Kindness

Kindness

This activity involves creating a daisy chain where each daisy represents one act of kindness.

Instructions:

1. Print and cut out the provided daisy flower shapes.

2. Have the kids write a specific act of kindness they've done, witnessed, or planned to do on each daisy petal, except for the "Kindness" petal.

3. Using glue or tape, attach the daisies, connecting the "Kindness" petals to form a chain.

4. Hang the daisy chain in a visible place and watch it grow as more acts of kindness are added.

Activity 4: Kindness Role-Play

Kids will engage in a role-play activity where they practice displaying kindness.

Instructions:

1. As a group or family, brainstorm various scenarios where kindness can be shown (e.g., helping someone carry groceries, standing up for someone being bullied, complimenting someone's work).

2. Assign roles to each participant and encourage them to act out the scenario, showing kindness in their actions and words.

3. After each scenario, discuss the importance of kindness and its impact on others.

Activity 5: Word Search: Acts of Kindness

R	F	E	L	S	H	A	R	E	K	Y	V
E	D	P	Q	M	Y	I	Z	V	Y	H	M
S	P	E	N	C	O	U	R	A	G	E	Q
P	F	O	R	G	I	V	E	V	U	D	R
E	Z	J	J	C	O	M	F	O	R	T	J
C	I	N	C	L	U	D	E	L	B	Q	T
T	C	T	B	G	L	I	S	T	E	N	R
W	H	C	Z	O	C	H	E	L	P	X	U

Find the following words in the puzzle.
Words are hidden ➡ and ⬇

COMFORT   INCLUDE

ENCOURAGE   LISTEN

FORGIVE   RESPECT

HELP   SHARE

Kids will complete a word search puzzle, finding words related to acts of kindness.

Instructions:

1. Provide the kids with the printable word search puzzle sheet.
2. Have the kids search for and circle the words related to acts of kindness.
3. Discuss the meaning of each word and its connection to kindness with the kids.

Activity 6: Kindness Bingo

ASK SOMEONE NEW TO PLAY AT RECESS	HOLD THE DOOR OPEN FOR SOMEONE	WRITE A KIND NOTE TO YOUR PARENTS	LET YOUR BROTHER/SISTER PLAY WITH YOUR TOYS	LEAVE A NOTE IN A LIBRARY BOOK
CLEAN UP YOUR ROOM WITHOUT BEING ASKED	DRAW A PICTURE AND GIVE IT TO A FRIEND	GIVE A HUG TO EACH MEMBER OF YOUR FAMILY	SAY THANK YOU TO THE BUS DRIVER	HOLD THE DOOR FOR SOMEONE
READ TO SOMEONE	CALL YOUR GRANDPARENTS JUST TO SAY HI		WOKE UP WITH A SMILE ON YOUR FACE	TELL SOMEONE THEY HAD A GOOD IDEA TODAY
TELL YOUR PARENTS YOU LOVE THEM	WRITE A KING NOTE TO YOUR TEACHER	PUT YOUR PLATE IN THE DISHWASHER	SAY "THANK YOU"	DONATE CLOTHES YOUT HAVE OUTGROWN
WRITE A KIND NOTE TO A CLASSMATE	PUR EVERY ITEM IN THE RECYCLING BIN	GIVE SOMEONE A COMPLIMENT	CHOOSE AN AREA TO PICK UP LITTER	TELL A JOKE TO A FRIEND

Kids will participate in a "Kindness Bingo" game to complete acts of kindness, aiming to get five on their bingo cards in a row.

Instructions:

1. Provide each child with a printable Kindness Bingo card.

2. Explain that the goal is to complete acts of kindness listed on the card to get five in a row, either vertically, horizontally, or diagonally.

3. When a child completes an act of kindness, they mark off the corresponding square on their card.

4. Encourage the kids to shout "Kindness Bingo!" once they have achieved five in a row.

5. Celebrate each "Kindness Bingo" and discuss the positive impact of the various acts of kindness.

Activity 7: Smile Challenge

1. *Challenge yourself to make someone smile!*

Source: https://unsplash.com/photos/hQNFPZK8F80

2. *In this challenge, kids will try to make others smile by using a kind gesture, compliment, or joke.*

Instructions:

1. Gather the kids and explain the Smile Challenge – to make others smile through acts of kindness.

2. Brainstorm various ways to make people smile, such as telling a funny joke, giving compliments, or helping out.

3. Encourage the kids to make as many people smile as possible throughout the day.

4. At the end of the day, discuss the various methods used to make people smile and the positive impact of spreading happiness.

Activity 8: Kindness Tree

Kindness TREE

Kids will create a Kindness Tree and add leaves representing their acts of kindness.

Instructions:

1. Draw or print a large tree trunk and branches on a piece of paper or poster board, leaving space for adding leaves.

2. Print and cut out the provided leaf shapes.

3. Have the kids write their acts of kindness on the leaves and then attach them to the tree branches.

4. Place the Kindness Tree in a visible spot, and encourage the kids to add leaves as they perform more acts of kindness.

5. As the tree fills with leaves, discuss the various acts of kindness and their positive impact.

Activity 9: Kindness Rocks

Kindness rocks.

Kids will paint and hide "Kindness Rocks" with positive messages or designs for others to find.

Steps:

1. Collect or purchase small, smooth rocks suitable for painting.

2. Provide paint, brushes, and other desired materials for decorating the rocks.

3. Encourage the kids to paint positive messages, designs, or pictures on the rocks.

4. Once the rocks have dried, go on a walk together to hide them in various locations for others to find, spreading kindness to those who discover them.

Activity 10: Letters of Appreciation

Kids will write letters of appreciation to people who have shown them kindness or made a difference in their lives.

Instructions:

1. Print the provided letter of appreciation template.

2. Discuss with the kids to whom they might want to write a letter, such as a teacher, coach, family member, or friend.

3. Encourage the kids to think about specific examples of kindness or support they have received from the person they are writing to and include these in their letters.

4. Once the letters are complete, help the kids mail or deliver them to their intended recipients.

Chapter 2: Encouraging Teamwork

"Coming together is a beginning, staying together is progress, and working together is a success." - Henry Ford

Teaching effective teamwork early on has numerous benefits for children's development and future success. By fostering collaboration and cooperation, children learn essential skills that will help them navigate various aspects of their lives, from school to the workplace. Teamwork is a vital skill for children to master, as it enables them to work effectively with others in their personal and professional lives. By encouraging healthy collaboration and cooperation, you are helping your child develop essential interpersonal competencies, such as empathy, compromise, and problem-solving. This chapter aims to provide engaging activities and exercises that promote teamwork and allow children to learn and practice these valuable skills. And with a mix of indoor and outdoor games tailored for different age groups, there's something for everyone.

Benefits of Encouraging Teamwork

Here are some primary benefits and psychological reasons behind promoting teamwork and collaboration in early childhood.

Social Skills Development

Teamwork requires children to interact with others, practice effective communication, and understand the perspectives of their peers. These social skills form a critical foundation for forming and maintaining relationships later in life. According to developmental psychologist Lev Vygotsky's sociocultural theory, social interaction is central to cognitive development. This means that learning how to work with others contributes to social skills and intellectual growth.

Emotional Intelligence

Teamwork helps children develop empathy, emotional regulation, and conflict-resolution skills. Collaborative activities require children to recognize and respond to the emotions of others, contributing to a better understanding of their feelings. A high level of emotional intelligence has been linked to better interpersonal relationships, higher academic performance, and increased well-being.

Problem-Solving and Critical Thinking

Participating in teamwork provides opportunities for children to solve problems together, think critically, and develop innovative solutions. When children collaborate, they pool their knowledge and resources, which enables them to approach challenges from different angles. This collective problem-solving process promotes critical thinking skills and fosters a growth mindset.

Responsibility and Accountability

Being part of a team means that children must take responsibility for their actions and contribute to the group's success. Early exposure to teamwork fosters a sense of accountability, teaching children that their decisions, actions, and inactions can impact others. Learning to be responsible and accountable at a young age can significantly contribute to their success in various facets of life.

Confidence and Self-Esteem

When children experience success in a team environment, they develop confidence in their abilities and gain a sense of accomplishment. Engaging in teamwork helps children recognize their strengths, understand the value they bring to a group, and develop a positive self-image.

Resilience and Adaptability

Teamwork allows children to face challenges, learn from failures, and adapt to changing situations. This resilience is an essential life skill that enables children to persevere and navigate obstacles in their future lives, whether in their academic or professional careers.

Preparing for the Future

In today's global and interconnected world, collaborating and working effectively within diverse teams is becoming increasingly important. By learning teamwork skills early, children are better prepared for the collaborative nature of today's workforce and higher education environments.

In conclusion, teaching effective teamwork at an early age fosters the development of vital social, emotional, cognitive, and interpersonal skills. These skills contribute to a child's success in various aspects of life, from academics to professional careers. Promoting teamwork and collaboration in early childhood sets the stage for our children to be compassionate, capable, and well-adjusted individuals.

Activities

Activity 11: Creating a Team Mural

Introducing a team mural activity is a fantastic way for children to develop communication, social skills, and artistic collaboration.

Instructions:

1. **Gather materials:** Large paper or canvas, various art supplies (paints, markers, crayons), tape, or adhesive for attaching the paper to the wall.

2. **Choose a theme:** Discuss with the children and decide on a theme or topic they want to represent in the mural.

3. **Designate work areas:** Give each child their designated space on the mural paper where they will create their part of the design.

4. **Encourage collaboration:** Have children discuss their ideas with one another and find ways to connect their pieces to create a cohesive design.

5. **Provide guidance:** Offer assistance when needed and encourage kids to communicate and work together while working on their sections of the mural.

6. **Allow time for completion:** Set aside ample time for children to complete their artwork without feeling rushed.

7. **Display and celebrate:** Once completed, display the mural in a prominent place where all participants can see it and appreciate their hard work as part of Indoor Teamworking Activities for Kids.

8. **Reflect on teamwork:** Lead a discussion about what they learned through this collaborative activity - how communication skills were important and how they had to cooperate throughout the process.

Activity 12: A Game of Charades

Introducing a game of charades to your kids is an excellent way to encourage teamwork and enhance communication skills.

Instructions:

1. **Gather your participants:** Divide the children into two or more teams with even numbers of players on each side.

2. **Prepare the words or phrases:** Create a list of age-appropriate words and phrases for children to act out during the game. You can tailor these to their interests or use general categories such as animals, movies, or books.

3. **Explain the rules:** Ensure that all participants understand the objective is to act out their given word or phrase without speaking while their teammates try to guess it.

4. **Take turns selecting words:** One member from each team will take turns drawing a word or phrase from the prepared list.

5. **Set a time limit:** Establish a reasonable time limit (e.g., 30 seconds) for each round, allowing adequate opportunities for acting and guessing within that time frame.

6. **Keep score:** Award points for each correct guess; consider offering bonus points if a team can successfully guess within a shorter timeframe than allotted.

7. **Celebrate success:** Congratulate all participants on their teamwork efforts and acknowledge individual achievements.

Activity 13: Capture the Flag

Playing Capture the Flag is fun for kids to practice teamwork and communication skills.

Instructions:

1. Divide players into two teams.
2. Each team should designate a home base where they will keep their flag.
3. The game's goal is for each team to capture the other team's flag and bring it back to their home base without getting tagged by an opponent.
4. Players can tag opponents by touching them or throwing a soft object like a foam ball.
5. When tagged, players must go to "jail," which is usually a designated spot on the other team's side of the playing area.
6. Players can be freed from jail if one of their teammates tags them without getting tagged themselves.
7. The game ends when one team successfully captures the other team's flag and returns it to their home base.

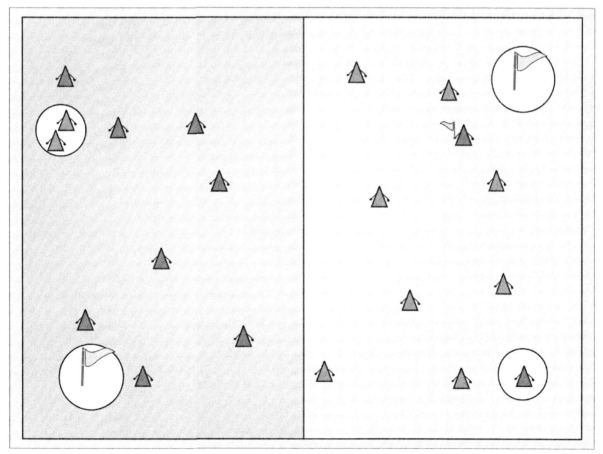

Activity 14: Save the Egg

Create a gadget that will protect an egg when dropped from a certain height.

Materials needed:

- Raw eggs
- Balloons
- Cardboard
- Paper
- Tape
- Scissors

Instructions:

1. Divide the participants into groups of 3-4.
2. Provide each group with the necessary materials.
3. Explain the goal of the activity: to protect the egg so it doesn't break when dropped from a certain height.
4. Allow groups 20 minutes to brainstorm and construct their egg-protecting contraptions.
5. Once time is up, test each contraption by dropping it from the selected height.
6. Discuss the results as a group, emphasizing the importance of teamwork, creativity, and problem-solving.

Activity 15: Marshmallow Challenge

Build the tallest structure using only a limited number of supplies.

Materials needed:

- Spaghetti
- Tape
- Marshmallows

Instructions:

1. Divide the participants into groups of 3-4.
2. Provide each group with the necessary materials.
3. Explain the goal of the activity: to build the tallest structure using only the provided materials.
4. Allow groups 20 minutes to construct their structures.
5. Once time is up, measure each structure to determine the winner.
6. Discuss the process and results as a group, emphasizing the importance of teamwork, planning, and adaptation.

Activity 16: Blindfold Obstacle Course

Navigate a blindfolded participant through an obstacle course with the guidance of their teammates.

Materials needed:

- Blindfolds
- Space to set up the obstacle course
- Cones or markers

Instructions:

1. Set up an obstacle course using cones or markers.
2. Divide the participants into groups of 2-3.
3. One group member will be blindfolded, while the other participants will guide them through the course using only verbal instructions.
4. The blindfolded participant will navigate the course with the help of their teammates.
5. Repeat the activity with each participant taking a turn as the blindfolded navigator.
6. Discuss the importance of trust, communication, and teamwork throughout the activity.

Activity 17: The Human Knot

Work together as a team to unravel the "knot" formed by holding each other's hands.

Instructions:

1. Have participants form a circle, standing close together.

2. Instruct each child to reach out and grab random hands across the circle, creating a knot.

3. Without letting go of each other's hands, the group must work together to untangle the knot and return to a standing circle.

4. Discuss the importance of communication, problem-solving, trust, and teamwork throughout the activity.

Activity 18: Hula Hoop Pass

Pass a hula hoop around a circle as quickly as possible without breaking handholds.

Instructions:

1. Have participants stand in a circle, holding hands.
2. Introduce the hula hoop into the circle by having one participant slide it onto their arm.
3. Explain the goal of the activity: pass the hula hoop around the circle without letting go of each other's hands.
4. Increase the challenge level without holding hands or introducing additional hula hoops.
5. Discuss the importance of strategy, coordination, and teamwork throughout the activity.

Activity 19: Trust Walk

Build trust between partners through a guided, blindfolded walk.

Instructions:

1. Pair participants up and select one participant as the guide and the other as the blindfolded walker.
2. Blindfold the walker and have the guide verbally guide them around a preselected area.
3. After successful completion, switch roles and repeat the activity.
4. Discuss the importance of trust, communication, and teamwork throughout the activity.

Activity 20: Maze Master

Improve teamwork, communication, and leadership skills by guiding a blindfolded team member through a maze on a workbook page.

Maze Master

Instructions:

1. Divide participants into pairs.
2. One participant will be the "guide," and the other will be the "navigator."
3. Provide each pair with a copy of the maze on a workbook page.
4. Blindfold the navigator and position them at the start of the maze.
5. The guide will give verbal instructions to help the blindfolded navigator trace a path through the maze using their finger.
6. Without touching the workbook, the guide must communicate effectively to help the navigator reach the finish line.
7. When the maze is completed, participants will switch roles and complete the activity again.
8. Discuss the importance of communication, teamwork, and trust during the activity.

Chapter 3: Enhancing Listening and Speaking Skills

"Effective communication is 20% what you know and 80% how you feel about what you know." - Jim Rohn

Communication is the key to building stronger relationships and achieving success in various aspects of life. As parents, it is crucial to help your child develop their speaking and listening skills, as these abilities are vital for their overall growth and development. This chapter aims to provide practical tips and techniques to assist you in nurturing these crucial skills within your child.

Active listening forms a cornerstone of efficient communication and is vital for constructing meaningful relationships as your child grows. Beginning from a young age, you should instill in your child the ability to focus on and genuinely comprehend other people's perspectives. This practice not only enhances their ability to respond appropriately but also promotes empathy, ensuring that they develop into dutiful listeners who can navigate social situations steadily and effectively.

Language development, central to the construction of robust communication skills, hinges upon vocabulary enrichment. This comes from a myriad of activities, from reading various genres of books together with your child, engaging them in enlightening conversations, to exposing them to new words and phrases as often as possible. The wider your child's vocabulary, the greater their ability to articulate thoughts, emotions, and ideas effectively and seamlessly. So, discovering the magical world of words together not only stimulates cognitive development but also facilitates unhampered verbal expression.

Cultivating the habit of asking questions in your child is another building block of effective communication. Clarifying queries can clear potential misunderstandings, deepen knowledge, and ensure the exchange is interactive. Nurture this critical behavior by modeling the practice of asking potent, open-ended questions and encouraging your child to replicate this when conversing.

While your child is making efforts to practice and improve their communication skills, ensure that your feedback is positive and constructive. Resorting to criticism can profoundly impact a child's self-esteem and penchant to learn. By adopting a supportive and harmonious approach, you can turn every communication attempt into a learning experience, heightening their confidence and fostering an environment of continued effort and improvement.

Confidence in communication comes with regular practice. Allow your child to experiment with various modes of communication – casual talking, formal phone conversations, or even public presentations. Begin with simpler tasks before proceeding to complex ones. Encourage them continually, reassuring them that it's perfectly okay to make mistakes along the way. As they venture beyond their comfort zones, they will gain the self-assurance to express themselves creatively and fearlessly.

Reflection is an integral part of learning. Once your child has taken part in a conversation or communication exercise, motivate them to introspect on the experience. Ask what they felt went well, what areas they think may need improvement, and what they learned from the process. This reflective practice will help them to identify their areas of strength and where they need to focus in the growth and enhancement of their communication abilities.

Benefits

1. **Academic Success:** Effective communication skills (including speaking and listening) contribute to a child's ability to understand and express ideas, leading to improved academic performance.

2. **Social Skills:** Reinforcing speaking and listening skills helps children develop better interpersonal connections, allowing them to form and maintain meaningful relationships with family, friends, and peers.

3. **Emotional Intelligence:** Enhancing speaking and listening skills bolsters children's ability to recognize, express, and manage emotions, paving the way for healthy emotional regulation and empathy.

4. **Critical Thinking:** Improved speaking and listening skills equip children with the tools to analyze, evaluate, and synthesize information, promoting essential critical thinking abilities.

5. **Confidence and Self-esteem:** When children are effective communicators, they can express themselves clearly and confidently, resulting in increased self-esteem and a greater sense of accomplishment.

6. **Career Success:** Mastering speaking and listening skills prepares children for future careers by enabling them to communicate ideas effectively, engage in successful negotiations, and work efficiently in team settings.

Activities

Activity 21: Colorful Storytelling

Instructions:

1. Grab your child's favorite coloring pencils together. Let's bring this story to life!

2. Encourage your child to color the characters and the speech bubbles while you read the story aloud.

3. You can also ask your child to imagine what the characters might be thinking and have them color the thought bubbles accordingly.

4. This activity will enhance their listening skills and spark their creativity!

Animal Sound Match

Instructions:

1. Let's have fun with animal sounds!
2. As you name each animal, ask your child to listen carefully and identify the sound it makes.
3. Then, fill in the empty sound bubbles with the correct sounds.
4. This activity will boost their listening skills and help them practice their speaking abilities!

Activity 23: Talking Puzzles

Talking Puzzles

Blue	Play	Where
Big	One	Tree
Down	Yellow	Help

Talking Puzzles

Where

Big

Blue

Help

Tree

Yellow

Down

One

Play

Instructions:

1. Let's solve some talking puzzles! Print this page and cut out the puzzle pieces.
2. Ask your child to listen carefully as you say each word aloud.
3. Together, try to find the matching puzzle pieces and assemble them correctly in the designated space.
4. This activity will enhance their listening and speaking skills and problem-solving abilities!

Rhyme Time

COW

- - - - - - - - - -

GOAT

- - - - - - - - - -

DONKEY

- - - - - - - - - -

PIG

- - - - - - - - - -

RABBIT

- - - - - - - - - -

ROOSTER

- - - - - - - - - -

HORSE

- - - - - - - - - -

SHEEP

- - - - - - - - - -

HEN

- - - - - - - - - -

Instructions:

1. Get ready for some rhyme time! Print this page and have your child color the cute animals.
2. Then, encourage them to listen attentively as you say the name of each item aloud.
3. Ask your child to think of a word that rhymes with the given name and write it in the blank space provided.
4. This activity will playfully enhance their listening, speaking, and literacy skills!

Following Directions

1. Join the lines to form the Rainbow.
2. Color the Rainbow with the missing colors.
3. Color the tractor red.
4. Color the pig.
5. Color the farmer's hat brown.
6. Color the farmer's clothes as desired.
7. Circle the little ducks.
8. Color the Cow.
9. Color the apples red.
10. Color the tree trunk brown.
11. Join the lines to form the sheep.
12. Color the leaf that the ant is holding.
13. Color the flowers.
14. Color the bird sitting on the tree.
15. Color the butterfly with different colors.
16. Color the sun Yellow.

Following Directions

Instructions:

1. Let's test your child's listening skills with a fun following directions activity!

2. Print this page and encourage your child to color the scene and its elements.

3. Read the instructions aloud, ask your child to listen carefully, and perform the actions with the corresponding elements.

4. This activity will help improve their listening comprehension and ability to follow instructions while having a playful and colorful experience!

Guess the Sound

Instructions:

1. Time to play "Guess the Sound!" Print this page and have your child color the adorable objects or animals.
2. Together, brainstorm and write down each item's sounds in the empty sound bubbles.
3. Once you have filled them all, take turns making the sounds while covering the bubbles.
4. See if your child can guess the correct sound by listening carefully.
5. This activity will enhance their listening skills and encourage their imagination!

Conversation Cards

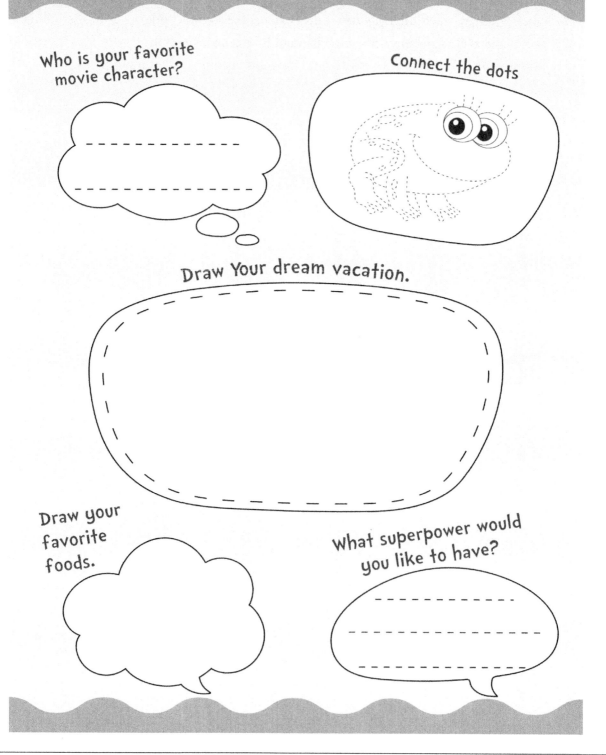

Who is your favorite movie character?

Connect the dots

Draw your dream vacation.

Draw your favorite foods.

What superpower would you like to have?

Instructions:

1. Let's have a conversation!
2. Print this page and have your child color the speech bubbles.
3. Encourage them to think about each prompt or question and respond by drawing or writing in the space provided.
4. Listen attentively to their responses and encourage them to elaborate as you engage in a conversation.
5. This activity will enhance their listening and speaking skills and ability to express themselves!

Instructions:

1. Print this page and have your child color the characters in the speech bubbles.

2. Start by whispering a simple sentence into your child's ear. Then, have them repeat the sentence to the next person, and so on.

3. As the sentence travels along the telephone wire, it might change slightly!

4. This activity will enhance their listening and speaking skills and their ability to pay attention and communicate clearly!

Activity 29: Story Building

Instructions:

1. Let's build a story together! Print this page and have your child color the story elements.

2. Ask your child to listen carefully as you take turns adding elements to the story. For example, you can start with a character and have your child choose a setting or an object to add.

3. Encourage them to use their imagination and describe their choices.

4. This activity will enhance their listening and speaking skills, as well as their creativity and storytelling abilities!

Activity 30: Word Hunt

Instructions:

1. Print this page and have your child color the lively scene.
2. Ask them to listen attentively as you call out different words hidden in the picture. Together, try to find and circle each word.
3. You can also challenge your child to pronounce or use the words in sentences.
4. This activity will enhance their listening, vocabulary, and speaking skills while having a playful and engaging experience!

Sound Charades

Instructions:

1. Print this page and have your child color the action illustrations.

2. Next, ask your child to listen carefully as you describe a sound or action without using words directly representing it.

3. For example, you can describe the sound of rain by saying, "Pitter-patter."

4. Then, your child can guess the sound or action and write or draw it in the space provided.

5. This activity will enhance their listening skills, creativity, and ability to interpret and communicate through non-verbal cues!

Instructions:

1. Print this page and have your child color the illustrations.
2. Encourage them to carefully observe each scene and think about what the characters might be saying or thinking.
3. Ask your child to fill in the empty speech bubbles or thought bubbles with their descriptions.
4. This activity will enhance their listening skills, imagination, and storytelling abilities, as well as their ability to express themselves through written or drawn communication!

Chapter 4: Practicing Gratitude

"Gratitude makes sense of our past, brings peace for today, and creates a vision for tomorrow." - Melody Beattie

It has been said that gratitude is the parent of all virtues. Being thankful and appreciative for the abundance of good fortune we receive in life is essential to leading a happy and fulfilling life. As parents and caregivers, it is critical to help children practice gratitude at an early age. Not only is gratitude an invaluable life skill, but it will also help kids manage their emotions and build better habits as they age. A strong foundation in gratitude from an early age has a basis in various psychological theories and is crucial for the emotional well-being of children.

The foundation of gratitude in children can be traced back to the seminal work of Lawrence Kohlberg's Theory of Moral Development (Kohlberg, 1971). His research showed that children develop cognitive and emotional skills that help them progress through different stages of moral understanding, including basic appreciation and being thankful. The earlier you start with gratitude practices, the more likely they will be ingrained in a child's emotional framework.

Another theory that supports the importance of gratitude in children is Social Learning Theory (Bandura, 1977). This theory posits that children learn by observing and mimicking the behaviors of others, such as parents, teachers, and peers. By consistently modeling and reinforcing gratitude in their everyday lives, parents can pave the way for children to adopt the same behavior and make it a habit as they grow older.

Benefits

Gratitude has numerous emotional and psychological benefits for children. According to Positive Psychology, gratitude can serve as armor against negative emotions and harmful mental health issues. Studies have found that cultivating gratitude early on can result in higher levels of subjective happiness, lower rates of depression and anxiety, more satisfying relationships, and increased resilience to stress (Emmons & McCullough, 2003; Wood et al., 2010).

Furthermore, gratitude has been linked to a growth mindset (Dweck, 2006), which believes that our abilities and intelligence can develop over time through effort and perseverance. By practicing gratitude, children can appreciate their achievements, learn from their mistakes, and remain optimistic about challenges.

Overcoming Obstacles to Teaching Gratitude to Children

Teaching gratitude to children is a challenging yet vital task for parents and educators. One of the foremost obstacles is the strong influence of society and peer pressure that fosters opposite values, such as entitlement and consumerism. Creating a supportive environment that encourages gratitude and appreciation is essential to overcome these obstacles. This can be achieved by consistently modeling grateful behavior, engaging children in discussions on gratitude, and providing opportunities for them to express and experience thankfulness. Encouraging children to participate in acts of kindness and volunteering can further help them develop empathy, understanding, and an attitude of gratitude. Most importantly, celebrating and reinforcing their efforts to show gratitude will give them the motivation and confidence to continue practicing this virtue.

Addressing Entitlement Mindset

The entitlement mindset can be a significant barrier to cultivating gratitude in children. To address this, parents and educators must set clear expectations, boundaries, and consequences for behavior. Ensuring that children understand the value of hard work, respect, and cooperation will help them appreciate their rights and privileges more deeply. In addition, nurturing children's emotional intelligence can help them become more aware of their feelings and better equipped to manage them, thus reducing the hold entitlement may have on them. Encourage children to reflect on their actions, appreciate the efforts of others, and recognize that they are not the center of the universe. Promoting empathy and humility can replace an entitlement mindset with gratitude and respect.

Navigating Over-Consumerism

In a world characterized by over-consumerism, children are often exposed to countless advertisements and messages that promote materialism. Social media influence fuels the fire by constantly creating unrealistic expectations and promoting the idea that happiness lies in the latest gadgets or fashion trends. To help children resist the lure of consumerism, parents and educators should encourage them to appreciate non-material values, such as love, kindness, and friendship. Discussing marketing tactics and teaching media literacy can help children become critical consumers and reduce their vulnerability to over-consumerism. Encouraging children to value experiences and relationships over material possessions, setting limits on shopping, and promoting responsible spending habits can further build their resistance to consumerism and reinforce the importance of gratitude.

Limiting Screen Time and Media Exposure

Excessive screen time and media exposure can significantly contribute to the erosion of gratitude within children as they become increasingly focused on their desires and less mindful of the feelings and needs of others. Parents and educators should establish and enforce limits on how much time children spend on screens and monitor the content they consume. Encouraging alternative activities that engage children in meaningful interactions with family, friends, and the surrounding environment can help them develop gratitude and emotional intelligence. Discussion of media content and its potential impact can empower children to think critically, filter out negative messages, and cultivate gratitude toward the positive aspects of their lives.

Activities for Young Children

Activity 33: Gratitude Jar

1. Start by explaining the concept of gratitude to the children. Teach them the importance of being thankful for the things and people in their lives.
2. Find a clear jar or container to collect notes throughout the year. Make sure it's big enough to hold lots of notes!
3. Decorate the jar together using stickers, paint, or markers. Write "Gratitude Jar" on it so everyone knows its purpose.
4. Place the jar in a common area where everyone can access it easily (e.g., the living room or kitchen).
5. Each day, encourage the children to write or draw something they are grateful for on a small piece of paper.
6. Fold the paper and place it in the jar.
7. Make it a family routine by sharing what each member wrote before adding their notes to the jar.
8. At the end of the year (or any chosen time), open the jar together and read the notes. This will remind everyone of what they were grateful for during the year.

Activity 34: Daily Gratitude Journal

1. Provide each child with a notebook or journal for their gratitude entries.
2. Create a consistent routine by setting aside time each day for journaling.
3. Encourage children to think about their day and write down at least one thing they are grateful for. It could be big or small, like enjoying a delicious meal or receiving help from a friend.
4. Review the entries occasionally to reflect on the positive things and experiences.
5. Keep the journals safe for future reflection and gratitude practice.

Thank-You Notes

1. Explain the importance of expressing gratitude to people who have helped or cared for the children.

2. Provide materials like cards, paper, markers, and stickers for creating thank-you notes.

3. Encourage children to write a thank-you note whenever they receive a gift, a kind gesture, or help from someone.

4. Help the children write thoughtful messages expressing their appreciation for the gift, assistance, or act of kindness.

5. Encourage children to give or send the thank-you notes personally to show their appreciation.

Activity 36: Gratitude Stones

1. Find several smooth stones or pebbles and clean them well.

2. Lay out craft materials like acrylic paint, markers, and brushes for decorating the stones.

3. Have children think about a word or phrase that represents something they are thankful for, like "family," "friends," or "health."

4. Help children paint or write their chosen word or phrase on the stone. Encourage creativity with the design!

5. Allow the stones to dry completely.

6. Place the stones where the children can see them daily as a visual reminder to be grateful for the things represented by each stone.

7. Encourage the children to hold or touch the stones whenever they need a reminder of what they are grateful for.

Activities for School Children

Activity 37: Gratitude Letter Writing

1. Explain the concept of gratitude letters to the children, emphasizing the importance of expressing appreciation for the impact someone has had on their lives.

2. Help the children brainstorm a list of people they would want to write a gratitude letter to, such as teachers, coaches, family members, or friends.

3. Provide materials like paper, pens, and envelopes for writing the letter.

4. Encourage the children to describe why they are grateful for the person and provide specific examples of how they have positively affected their lives.

5. Assist the children in checking their letters for clarity, proper grammar, and spelling.

6. Teach the children how to properly address and mail the letter if needed, or encourage them to hand-deliver it in person.

Volunteering at a Local Charity or Shelter

1. Research local charities, shelters, or nonprofit organizations that allow children to volunteer.

2. Discuss the different volunteer opportunities with the children to find which ones they are most interested in.

3. Contact the chosen organization to schedule a day and time for volunteering, providing the necessary information and filling out any required forms.

4. Prepare the children beforehand by discussing the type of work they will be doing and reminding them of the importance of helping others.

5. Attend the volunteer event with the children, actively participating and showcasing gratitude for the opportunity to help others.

6. After the volunteering, discuss with the children the impact they made and the appreciation they gained for what they have.

Activity 39: Random Acts of Kindness

1. Teach children the importance of kindness and how random acts can positively affect others.

2. Sit down with the children and brainstorm a list of random acts of kindness they can perform, such as holding a door open, helping someone carry their groceries, or leaving a kind note for a neighbor.

3. Encourage the children to perform these acts of kindness regularly without expecting anything in return.

4. Discuss their experiences with random acts of kindness, emphasizing the positive feelings of helping others.

5. Praise the children for their kindness and explain how they are a form of gratitude toward others.

Activity 40: Family Gratitude Circle

1. Call a family meeting or gathering with the children and other family members.

2. Explain the concept of a gratitude circle, where everyone takes a turn sharing what they are grateful for.

3. Encourage each family member to gather in a circle, sitting or standing comfortably.

4. Choose someone to go first, then go clockwise around the circle, allowing each person to share what they are grateful for.

5. Urge the children to actively listen and express support for the other family members as they share their thoughts.

6. Discuss the benefits of expressing gratitude regularly and encourage the children to continue practicing it daily.

Activity 41: Handwritten Thank You Letters

1. Explain the significance of handwritten thank-you letters and why they are a meaningful way to express gratitude.

2. Guide children in thinking about a recent situation where someone provided a service, gift, or support that deserves a thank-you letter.

3. Provide materials like paper, pens, envelopes, and stamps for writing thank-you letters.

4. Help children write their letters, focusing on specific details about the service, gift, or support provided and expressing their appreciation authentically.

5. Assist the children in checking their letters for proper grammar and spelling.

6. Encourage the children to mail or hand-deliver their thank-you letters, teaching them how to address envelopes properly and apply postage if necessary.

Activity 42: Gratitude Tree

Gratitude Tree

Instructions:

1. Sit down with your child and explain the concept of gratitude. Talk about things they are grateful for, such as family, friends, pets, or favorite activities.

2. Encourage your child to write or draw one thing they are grateful for on each leaf. Help them if needed.

3. Once the leaves are ready, let your child place them on the tree branches, sticking them with glue or simply tucking them in the empty spaces.

4. As you and your child work together, discuss the reasons behind their gratitude and share your examples.

5. Display the completed Gratitude Tree in a prominent place in your home, such as on a wall or refrigerator. This will serve as a visual reminder of what you both appreciate.

Remember to express gratitude regularly to instill this positive value in your child's daily life.

Activity 43: Thankful Journal

Name: _____

date: _____

Name: _____

Name: ---------------------------------- date: ----------------

Instructions:

1. Explain to your child that this journal is a special place where they can write or draw things they are grateful for. Help them understand that it's a way to remember and appreciate the positive aspects of their lives.

2. Set aside a specific time each day or week to sit down with your child and reflect on what they are grateful for.

3. Encourage your child to write or draw about their experiences, people they appreciate, or things that bring them joy. They can use words and sentences or create small doodles representing gratitude.

4. Celebrate and discuss their entries together, fostering appreciation and positivity.

5. Keep the Thankful Journal safe, and encourage your child to revisit it whenever they need a reminder of the good things in their life.

Chapter 5: Manage Your Feelings

"Your emotions are the slaves to your thoughts, and you are the slave to your emotions." - Elizabeth Gilbert

Managing feelings in children is a crucial aspect of their emotional development and plays a significant role in their overall well-being. Helping children learn to recognize, express, and regulate their emotions enables them to develop healthy coping mechanisms and build strong social skills, which are essential for their success in later life.

Attachment theory, developed by John Bowlby and Mary Ainsworth, emphasizes the importance of a secure, nurturing relationship with their primary caregiver during early childhood. According to this theory, when children feel safe and supported, they are more likely to develop the ability to manage their emotions effectively.

Importance

Teaching emotional regulation to children is crucial for their overall well-being and development. Emotional intelligence, which encompasses self-awareness, empathy, and the ability to manage one's emotions, plays a significant role in shaping a child's success in various aspects of life – including academics, relationships, physical health, and mental wellness.

One prime example of the impact of emotional regulation is its influence on social skills. As kids learn to identify feelings and better understand others' perspectives through empathy exercises or group activities emphasizing cooperation and communication, they'll be better equipped to navigate daily interactions with friends or classmates.

Furthermore, teaching kids how to engage in stress management practices such as mindfulness techniques or deep-breathing exercises benefits them emotionally while equipping them with healthy coping mechanisms as they age.

These strategies give children the tools to handle challenging situations effectively without resorting to negative behaviors like acting out or withdrawing from others when overwhelmed by strong emotions.

Understanding Emotional Development in Children

Recognizing signs of emotional distress in kids is crucial to promoting healthy emotional development.

The Significance of Emotional Development

The significance of emotional development in children cannot be overstated, as it plays a pivotal role in shaping their psychological and social well-being. Healthy emotional growth allows children to build strong foundations for self-awareness, empathy, resilience, and effective communication skills.

For instance, consider a child who encounters bullying at school. If they have been equipped with the tools for understanding and regulating their emotions – thanks to supportive parents or caregivers – they are more likely to cope effectively by expressing their feelings without resorting to aggression or withdrawing from social situations altogether.

Factors That Affect It

Many factors can influence a child's emotional development, making it crucial for parents and caregivers to be aware of these factors when guiding children toward healthy emotional regulation. The key factors include:

1. **Child development:** Each stage of child development comes with unique developmental milestones, affecting their ability to understand and process emotions.

2. **Emotional regulation:** A child's natural ability to manage their emotions significantly helps them develop emotional skills over time.

3. **Social interactions:** The quality and quantity of social interactions contribute to developing a child's emotional intelligence and understanding of appropriate emotional responses.

4. **Genetics:** Genes can predispose children to specific traits, such as temperament, influencing their ability to regulate emotions.

5. **Cultural influences:** Different cultures have distinct beliefs about expressing and managing emotions, shaping a child's attitude towards emotional regulation.

6. **Life skills:** Developing essential life skills like communication, problem-solving, and coping strategies helps children better deal with emotionally challenging situations.

7. **Emotional intelligence:** Awareness and understanding of one's own emotions and those of others play a critical role in helping children manage feelings effectively.

8. **Personal growth:** A supportive environment that encourages personal growth can promote the development of strong emotional management skills in children.

9. **Societal outcomes:** Broad societal expectations about acceptable behavior can shape how kids are expected to express themselves emotionally within the larger community.

By considering these factors, parents and caregivers can create a nurturing environment that fosters positive emotional development for their kids and helps them succeed socially and emotionally throughout their lives.

Recognizing Signs of Emotional Distress in Kids

Sometimes, it can be difficult to recognize when a child is experiencing emotional distress, but it's essential to identify these signs early on. Kids who need help may become more withdrawn or irritable than usual, have trouble sleeping, lose interest in activities they once enjoyed, or even begin acting out aggressively toward others.

Other red flags might include sudden changes in eating habits, weight loss/gain, and academic struggles. As caregivers and parents, creating an environment that encourages honest conversations about mental health and well-being is important so children feel comfortable sharing their concerns with trusted adults.

Activities

Activity 44: Breathing Exercises with Visualization

Breathing exercises with visualization can be used as effective self-regulation strategies for kids. Visualization is a technique that helps bring awareness to the mind-body connection and can help kids regulate their emotions.

Here are some breathing exercises with visualization for kids:

1. **Take Five Breathing:** Inhale, hold your breath while counting to five, exhale while counting to five, and hold your breath while counting to five. Repeat.
2. **Balloon Breathing:** Imagine blowing up a balloon with your breath and letting it deflate slowly as you exhale.
3. **Ocean Breathing:** Inhale deeply through your nose and exhale slowly through your mouth like the sound of ocean waves crashing on the shore.
4. **Bunny Breath:** Inhale quickly through your nose with bunny sniffs and then exhale slowly through your mouth like a bunny, gently blowing kisses.
5. **Rainbow Breathing:** Imagine inhaling the colors of the rainbow and exhaling dark clouds or negative thoughts.

Breathing exercises with visualization are simple yet powerful tools that can help children manage their feelings better by bringing attention to their breathing patterns. Encourage them to practice these techniques when they feel stressed or overwhelmed, or incorporate them into daily routines such as bedtime or before starting homework.

Activity 45: Mindfulness Exercises

Teaching mindfulness exercises to your child can be an effective way of managing emotions. Here are some exercises you can try with guided instruction:

1. **Body scan meditation:** Start by asking your child to lie down and close their eyes. Have them take deep breaths and focus on each part of their body, slowly scanning from head to toe.
2. **The gratitude game:** Ask your child to name three things they are grateful for every day. This helps shift focus from negative thoughts to positive ones.
3. **Mindful breathing:** Teach your child to focus on their breathing when they feel overwhelmed or anxious. Encourage them to breathe in deeply through their nose and exhale slowly through their mouth.

4. **Mindful eating:** Encourage your child to eat mindfully, paying attention to the taste, texture, and smell of each bite.

5. **Loving-kindness meditation:** Have your child close their eyes and repeat positive affirmations like "May I be happy" or "May I be kind."

Activity 46: Mindfulness Activities with a Calendar

One effective way to incorporate mindfulness exercises into your child's daily routine is by using a calendar. Here are some activities you can include in your child's calendar:

1. Start each day with a gratitude exercise, encouraging your child to reflect on what they are thankful for.

2. Schedule 5 - 10 minutes of mindful breathing exercises each morning and evening.

3. Include a short-guided meditation session once or twice a week.

4. Plan a sensory activity once a week, such as coloring or listening to calming music.

5. Schedule outdoor time each day to encourage physical activity and connection with nature.

6. Set aside time for self-reflection and journaling at least once a week.

7. Incorporate yoga or stretching exercises into the weekly schedule for physical and mental relaxation.

8. Encourage acts of kindness towards others by scheduling volunteer activities or random acts of kindness days once a month.

By using a calendar, children can have structure in their mindfulness practice and better understand the importance of emotional regulation in their everyday lives.

Activity 47: Creating a Calming Corner

Creating a calming corner is an effective way to support emotional regulation in children. Here are some ideas for parents and caregivers to get started:

1. Choose a quiet, comfortable space in the home where the child can go to calm down and regulate their emotions.

2. Decorate the area with soft lighting, comfortable seating, and calming decorations like plants or artwork.

3. Provide tools like stress balls, fidget toys, or a weighted blanket that the child can use to self-soothe when feeling overwhelmed.

4. Keep items like books or puzzles nearby that the child can engage with to help distract from negative emotions.

5. Encourage the child to take deep breaths and practice mindfulness techniques in this space when they are feeling upset.

Activity 48: Sensory Activities

Sensory activities are a great way for children to regulate their emotions and manage feelings. Encourage your child to engage in these fun sensory exercises:

1. Create a sensory bin filled with rice, beans, or sand for your child to dig and play in.

2. Provide textured materials like slime or playdough for your child to squeeze and mold.

3. Use aromatherapy essential oils in a diffuser or cotton ball for your child to smell.

4. Offer tactile objects like stress balls or fidget spinners for your child to hold and manipulate.

5. Play music or use sound machines with calming sounds like waves crashing or birds chirping.

Activity 49: Anger Journaling with Prompts

One effective activity for managing anger in kids is to keep an anger journal. Here are some prompts to get your child started:

1. Write about a time when you felt angry and what caused it.

_____

_____

_____

Draw a picture of how you feel when you're angry.

2. Write down three things that help you calm down when you're feeling angry.

_____

_____

_____

3. Describe a situation where someone made you angry, but you could handle it calmly.

_____

_____

_____

4. Write about a time when you felt proud of yourself for managing your anger.

_____

_____

_____

Anger journaling can help children clear their minds and better understand the situations that trigger their anger. By reflecting on their emotions and behaviors, kids can build healthier coping skills and take control of their emotions.

Activity 50: Creating a Calm-Down Kit

Creating a calm-down kit can help children manage their emotions during stress and anger. Here are some items to include in the kit:

- Stress balls or fidget toys to keep hands busy
- A favorite stuffed animal or toy for comfort
- Earplugs or earmuffs to block out noise
- Bubble wrap for popping
- Snacks like fruit snacks or granola bars for when hunger strikes
- Sensory bottles filled with glitter, water, and beads for calming visual stimulation
- Coloring books and crayons for creative expression
- Positive affirmations written on index cards to repeat aloud
- Breathing exercises visualized on a card or sheet
- Worry dolls or worry stones for fidgeting and calming worries

Remember to personalize the kit with items that work best for your child's interests and needs to ensure optimal effectiveness in calming down during heightened emotional states.

Activity 51: Emotion Color Wheel

Instructions:

1. This interactive game will help your child understand and manage their feelings.

2. Start by explaining the different emotions represented on the wheel, such as happiness, sadness, anger, and excitement.

3. Encourage your child to choose a color for each emotion and fill in the sections with their favorite colors. After coloring, ask them to spin the arrow and name a situation that would make them feel the emotion the arrow points to.

4. Discuss these scenarios together and help your child explore positive ways to cope with different feelings.

Activity 52: Feeling Faces Collage

Feeling Faces Collage

Instructions:

1. Help your child express their emotions through art.

2. Start by cutting out the various facial features and expressions provided.

3. Let your child choose the facial features that best represent their current mood and arrange them on the blank canvas.

4. Encourage them to get imaginative and create funny or exaggerated faces, too! Once the collage is complete, help them stick it on the frame or backdrop.

5. This activity allows your child to explore different emotions playfully and artistically.

Activity 53: Emotion Puppet Show

Emotion Puppet Show

Instructions:

1. Start by introducing the different puppets and their emotions.

2. Encourage your child to color and decorate the puppets, making them unique and personal.

3. Once the puppets are ready, set up a stage or backdrop and guide your child in putting on a puppet show.

4. Let them act out different emotions using the puppets and ask questions to spark conversations about how they relate to the characters' feelings.

5. This activity promotes empathy and helps your child express and understand their own emotions.

Activity 54: Feelings Memory Game

Instructions:

    1. This activity will help your child recognize and match different emotions.

    2. Print and start by shuffling the cards and placing them face-down on a table or floor.

    3. Take turns flipping two cards over to find a matching emotion pair. When a match is found, encourage your child to talk about a time they felt that particular emotion.

    4. This game improves memory skills and helps your child understand that everyone experiences different feelings. Have fun playing and exploring emotions together!

Activity 55: Emotion Diary

Weather:

I feel:

My Drawing

IMPORTANT

NOTE:

WEDNESDAY

Weather:

I feel:

My Drawing

NOTE:
....
....
....
....
....
....

THURSDAY

Weather:

I feel:

My Drawing

NOTE:

_____

_____

_____

_____

_____

_____

FRIDAY

Weather:

I feel:

My Drawing

NOTE:

Weather: ☀ ⛅ ☁ ☁ 🌧 🌨 ⛈ 🌧 🌫 🌙 🌩 🌨 🌧 🌨

I feel: 😐 🙂 😣 😅 😤 😌 😳 😍 😶 😁 😫 😋 😈

My Drawing

NOTE:

Weather:

I feel:

My Drawing

NOTE:

Instructions:

1. This is a great way for your child to reflect on their emotions and experiences.

2. Give them their own diary and explain how it can be used to track their feelings. Encourage them to draw or write about their emotions each day, highlighting the events or situations that influenced their mood.

3. Remind them that having different feelings is okay and that the diary is a safe space to express themselves.

4. Make it a habit to sit down with your child and discuss their entries, offering support and guidance.

5. This activity fosters emotional awareness and encourages open communication between you and your child.

Activity 57: Emotion Charades

Emotion Charades

ROUND 1

Player/Team:

Player/Team:

ROUND 2

Player/Team:

Player/Team:

Emotion Charades

Instructions:

1. This activity will help your child practice recognizing and expressing emotions through movement.

2. Start by explaining the different emotions represented on the cards. Place them in a container or bag.

3. Take turns drawing a card and acting out the emotion without using any words. Encourage your child to observe your facial expressions and body language to guess the correct emotion.

4. Let them take a turn acting out emotions while you guess.

5. Keep score or record each successful guess to make it more exciting.

6. This playful activity promotes empathy and enhances your child's ability to understand and interpret emotions.

Activity 58: Feelings Collage

Instruction:

1. This hands-on project allows your child to express their emotions through art.

2. Start by explaining the different emotions and their corresponding sections on the collage template.

3. Gather a variety of colorful materials, such as magazines, colored paper, fabric, and stickers.

4. Encourage your child to search for images or materials representing each emotion and glue them onto the respective sections.

5. As they create the collage, ask them to talk about why they chose each material and how it relates to the specific emotion. This activity promotes self-expression and visual representation of feelings.

Feelings Collage

Instructions:

1. This activity allows your child to explore emotions through storytelling and creativity.

2. Start by introducing the emotion cards and the different scenarios they represent. Let your child choose a card and use it as inspiration for a story.

3. Provide them with a blank storybook template and encourage them to illustrate and write their own narrative.

4. They can use colorful stickers or illustrations to enhance their story. After completing the story, read it together and discuss the emotions and lessons learned from the characters' experiences.

5. This activity nurtures imagination, language skills, and emotional understanding.

Parenting Tips for Supporting Emotional Development

Encouraging healthy emotional expression and modeling emotional regulation are helpful tips for supporting your child's emotional development - learn more in this comprehensive guide.

Modeling Emotional Regulation

It is crucial to model emotional regulation as a parent or caregiver. Children learn by example, and seeing you healthily managing strong emotions helps them understand how to do the same.

Modeling emotional regulation means identifying and expressing your feelings appropriately and actively coping with challenging situations. Your children notice and learn from your behavior when you take deep breaths or count to 10 before reacting negatively.

By modeling emotional regulation for your child, you provide them with valuable skills to help them succeed socially and academically. Studies have found that children who experience positive parenting styles, like those that emphasize modeling good behavior, show stronger self-control and higher levels of empathy towards others than their peers who don't receive this support at home.

Creating a Safe and Supportive Home Environment

Parents and caregivers must create a safe and supportive home environment that promotes emotional well-being in children. One way to accomplish this is by modeling healthy emotional regulation, which can be achieved through active listening, empathizing with their feelings, and using age-appropriate language when discussing emotions.

Additionally, providing outlets for children to express themselves creatively without fear of judgment or criticism can help foster a positive emotional climate.

Establishing clear, consistently enforced boundaries is another important factor in creating a safe home environment. This provides structure and teaches children about responsibility and accountability while promoting independence within safe limits.

It's also essential to encourage open communication between family members, being careful not to dismiss or belittle their concerns, even if they seem trivial or insignificant.

Encouraging the Healthy Expression of Emotions

As parents and caregivers, it's essential to encourage children to express their emotions healthily. Children need to know that all emotions are valid and natural, and it's okay to express them.

One way of doing this is by creating a safe space where your child can talk about their feelings without fear of judgment or punishment.

Another way is through modeling. Parents can show their children how to manage emotions healthily by expressing theirs constructively. For example, instead of yelling when frustrated, take deep breaths or step away until ready to respond calmly.

Chapter 6: Respectful Role Playing to Build Boundaries

"Establishing and respecting personal boundaries is an act of self-care and self-respect." - Jane Smith

Teaching children about healthy boundaries and positive interactions with others is crucial for their emotional development. Role-playing is an effective tool to help them learn and practice these skills while having fun. Through different scenarios, kids can understand the importance of respecting personal space, appreciating diversity and culture, and developing assertive communication practices.

Importance of Teaching Respect, Healthy Boundaries, and Positive Interactions With Others

Teaching respect, healthy boundaries, and positive interactions with others are critical to raising well-rounded children. As parents and caregivers, it's essential to prioritize these values from an early age as they contribute significantly to your child's emotional development and intelligence.

Children who learn about healthy boundaries are better equipped to maintain strong relationships. A key component of this learning involves understanding physical boundaries and respecting personal space – whether it be other people's bodies or belongings.

Incorporating activities that nurture these values into your child's early childhood education prepares them for personal and professional future success. Respectful role-playing scenarios serve as engaging tools that allow kids to learn and practice vital life skills.

Role-Playing as an Effective Tool for Learning and Practicing These Skills

Role-playing is a powerful and engaging method to help children learn and practice essential life skills such as respecting boundaries, developing empathy, and improving communication.

By immersing themselves in realistic scenarios, kids can experiment with different strategies for handling situations that may arise in their day-to-day lives.

One example of role-playing activities involves teaching children about personal space and consent. In this scenario, parents or caregivers can encourage kids to pretend they are meeting new people at school or a community event.

By offering guidance on how to greet someone politely while respecting their physical boundaries, the child gains valuable experience in navigating social interactions safely and respectfully.

The experiential nature of role-play ensures that these lessons resonate more profoundly with children than merely listening to lectures or reading about appropriate behavior.

Related Theories

Role-playing activities draw inspiration from several key theories in child development and psychology, providing a strong foundation for teaching essential life skills. One such theory is the social learning theory, which emphasizes the importance of observing and imitating others to acquire new behaviors.

Another influential concept is play-based learning, which highlights the benefits of engaging children in fun and interactive experiences that foster cognitive growth and emotional intelligence.

As kids act out different scenarios during role-playing games, they strengthen communication skills while gaining insights into various cultural norms and societal expectations.

This active involvement helps them internalize concepts like personal space more effectively than passive lessons could achieve alone.

Personal Space and Consent Activities

This section will explore fun and engaging role-playing activities that teach children the importance of respecting personal space and understanding consent.

Definition of Personal Space and its Significance

Teaching your child the concept of personal space is essential for fostering healthy relationships and ensuring their safety. Personal space refers to the physical boundaries we create around ourselves, which vary from person to person.

It's an invisible buffer zone that helps maintain comfort, especially when interacting with others.

A strong grasp of personal space helps children develop social skills and navigate various situations without inadvertently causing discomfort or anxiety.

For example, a child who understands personal space will know not to hug a stranger or stand too close behind someone in line at school. Also, recognizing these boundaries allows kids to establish a sense of privacy and control over their bodies while respecting other people's limits.

Activity 60: "Respecting Personal Space"

Materials needed:

- Personal Space worksheet (included below)
- Pencils or crayons for drawing
- Pieces of yarn or string, 2-3 feet long, for each child

Preparation:

1. Print the Personal Space worksheet, providing one for each child.
2. Prepare pictures of people interacting in various social situations, showing respectful and disrespectful personal space behavior.

Activity Steps:

1. Explain to the children what "personal space" means. Personal space is the area around each person where they feel comfortable. If someone else is too close, they might feel uncomfortable or unsafe.

2. Use the pictures to discuss social situations where people's personal space might be respected or disrespected. Show examples of appropriate personal space, like standing in line at the grocery store or sitting in a classroom. Also, show examples of inappropriate personal space, like standing too close to someone while talking or sitting on someone's lap without permission.

3. Pass out the pieces of yarn or string to each child. Ask them to stand up and hold one end of the string in one hand and then use their other hand to pull the string out to form a circle around them. Explain that this circle represents their personal space.

4. Have the children walk around the room with their "personal space bubbles." Encourage them to pay attention to how closely they are standing with their friends. Discuss how it feels when someone is too close, and remind them that it's important to respect others' personal space.

5. Give each child a Personal Space worksheet. Have them draw two pictures - one where they are showing respect for someone's personal space and one where they are not. Have them write a sentence describing the situation and how it could be handled better next time.

6. Once the children have completed their worksheets, gather the group and have a few volunteers share their drawings. Discuss the situations and the importance of respecting personal space.

7. Summarize the activity by reminding the children that everyone has a personal space bubble. Encourage them to be aware of their own and others' personal space and to always show respect.

Personal Space Worksheet:

Draw a picture of a situation where you are respecting someone's personal space:

Write a sentence describing the situation:

_____

_____

_____

Draw a picture of a situation where you are not respecting someone's personal space:

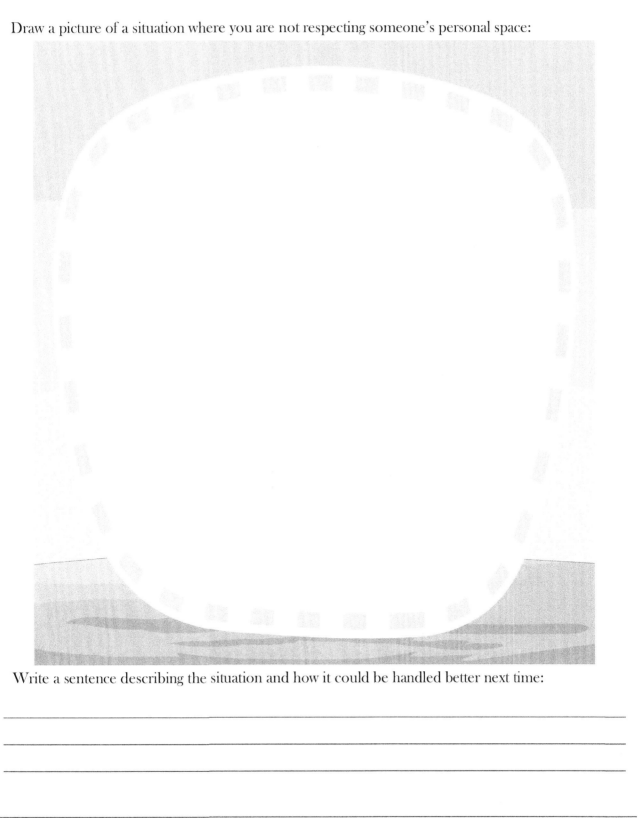

Write a sentence describing the situation and how it could be handled better next time:

_____

_____

_____

Activity 61: Personal space bubbles

Materials needed:

- Large sheet of paper and colored markers or crayons

Instructions:

1. Lay the large sheet of paper on the floor or table.
2. Ask your child to draw big circles on the paper.
3. Discuss the concept of personal space, using bubbles as a metaphor. Explain that when we step inside someone's bubble, we enter their personal space and need permission.
4. Ask your child to write or draw an example of respecting personal space inside a bubble. For example, waiting for an invitation to hug, stepping back when someone seems uncomfortable, or asking before playing with someone's hair.

Activity 62: Community Helper Role Play

Materials Needed:

- Different uniforms or costume pieces relating to various community jobs (fireman, policeman, doctor, teacher, etc.)
- Relevant props (like doctor's kit, fake money, classroom blackboard, etc.)

Instructions:

1. Discuss with your child the different helpers we have in our community and their roles. Explain how these individuals contribute to society.
2. Lay out the uniforms or costume pieces clearly visible for your child to understand. Place the corresponding props alongside each uniform.
3. Encourage your child to select a role they want to play. They can put on the costume and use the props associated with the chosen community helper.
4. Begin the role play with your child; you can be a citizen needing help, and your child will be the community helper. Make sure to ask questions and make statements that reinforce their understanding of the specific role.
5. Switch roles after a while for variety and an equal chance at experiencing the different jobs.
6. Use this activity to build your child's understanding of community helpers but also to educate them about the importance of helping others, teamwork, and appreciation for various professions.

(Please note: You can also incorporate other roles according to your child's interests, such as a chef, artist, athlete, etc.)

Activity 63: Role-Playing Asking for Permission

Instructions:

1. Create scenarios where your child can practice asking for permission before touching someone. You can use stuffed animals or action figures as participants.

2. Examples of situations could include asking permission to hug a friend, asking before borrowing a toy, or checking if holding hands during a game is okay.

3. Encourage your child to communicate clearly and respect the other participant's response, whether "yes" or "no."

Activity 64: "Celebrating Differences"

Teaching kids acceptance and appreciation for diversity is important in building a respectful and inclusive community. Here are five activities to help celebrate differences:

1. Introduce different cultures through food, music, dance, and clothing. Encourage kids to share their own cultural experiences and learn from others.

2. Assign each child a unique trait or characteristic, such as hair color or a favorite animal. Have them share why they appreciate that trait about themselves and how it adds value to the group.

3. Read books highlighting diverse characters or featuring cultural celebrations and discuss what can be learned from the stories.

4. Organize a cultural fair where kids can interactively present their family traditions, language, or history.

5. Challenge the idea of "normal" by discussing how everyone's differences make them special and deserving of respect.

By celebrating diversity, we can teach our kids tolerance, empathy, and inclusion while building stronger communities.

Activity 65: "Handling Prejudice"

Teaching your child how to handle prejudice is important in building boundaries and respect toward others. Here are some activities you can try with your child:

1. **Acknowledge the experience:** It's important to listen to your child when they share experiences of prejudice or discrimination. Validate their feelings and let them know it's okay to feel upset.

2. **Identify unfairness:** Discuss with your child what unfairness looks like, such as excluding someone because of their race or gender. Give examples and ask them how they would feel in that situation.

3. **Encourage empathy:** Help your child understand what it feels like to be discriminated against by encouraging them to put themselves in someone else's shoes.

4. **Practice assertiveness:** Teach your child to stand up for themselves and others respectfully when faced with prejudice or discrimination.

5. **Educate on diversity:** Teach your child about different cultures, religions, and backgrounds so that they can appreciate diversity and differences among individuals.

Assertive Communication Practices

Assertive communication is an important life skill that helps children express their feelings and resolve conflicts.

Explanation of Assertive Communication and its Benefits

Assertive communication is an essential skill that kids can learn and apply daily. It involves expressing oneself respectfully while being honest about one's feelings, needs, and boundaries.

There are many benefits to using assertive communication. For example, it helps to reduce anxiety and stress associated with difficult conversations or situations where healthy boundaries may be challenged.

Another significant benefit of assertiveness is that it empowers individuals by giving them more control over their lives.

In conclusion, teaching children the importance of assertive communication builds their confidence and equips them with essential life skills needed for successful social interactions.

Activity 66: "Expressing Feelings"

Teaching children how to express their feelings assertively can be challenging, but it is essential for building healthy boundaries and positive interactions with others. Here are some activities you can use to help your child practice assertive communication:

1. Have your child identify a situation where they would like to express their feelings assertively, such as when someone takes one of their toys without asking.

2. Ask your child to role-play the situation with you, taking turns playing themselves and the other person involved.

3. Encourage your child to use "I" statements to express their feelings clearly and directly, such as saying, "I feel upset when you take my toy without asking."

4. Help your child practice active listening by repeating back what the other person said before responding. For example, "So you're saying you wanted to play with my toy too?"

5. After the role-play exercise, ask your child how they felt about assertively expressing their feelings and if they thought it was an effective communication method.

By practicing assertive communication in a safe environment through role-playing exercises like this, children can develop better emotional regulation skills, build stronger relationships based on mutual respect and understanding, and grow into confident communicators who stand up for themselves and others when necessary.

Activity 67: "Resolving Conflict"

Learning how to resolve conflict is essential for kids to learn as they grow and develop relationships with others. By practicing assertive communication, children can work through disagreements while still respecting the feelings and boundaries of others. Here are some tips for helping kids learn how to resolve conflict:

1. **Encourage kids to express their feelings:** When children are upset or hurt by something that someone else has said or done, they need to be able to talk about their emotions clearly and respectfully.

2. **Teach problem-solving skills:** Help kids think through possible solutions to a conflict and consider the consequences of each option before coming to a resolution.

3. **Practice active listening:** Encourage children to listen carefully to what others say and understand where they are coming from before responding.

4. **Avoid aggressive or passive behavior:** Children should learn to stand up for themselves without resorting to aggression and avoid being passive and letting others walk over them.

5. **Work towards a win-win solution:** In most cases, conflict resolution involves compromise and finding a solution that works well for both parties.

By teaching kids these skills early on, we can help them build healthy relationships with friends, family members, and classmates as they grow up.

Activity 68: "My Bubble, My Space"

Instructions:

1. Begin by explaining the concept of personal boundaries to your child. Help them understand that personal boundaries are like an invisible bubble around them that represents their personal space and feelings.

2. Introduce the activity page to your child.

3. Encourage your child to color the bubble with their favorite colors and decorate it however they like.

4. Inside the bubble, ask your child to draw or write things that make them feel happy, comfortable, and safe. These could include activities they enjoy, people they trust, or anything that brings them joy.

5. On the outer edges of the bubble, ask your child to draw or write things that make them uncomfortable, scared, or upset. These could include situations they want to avoid or actions they don't like.

6. Take some time to discuss the completed page with your child. Ask them to explain their choices and feelings. Emphasize respecting their boundaries and recognizing when others should respect them, too.

Activity 69: "Respecting Boundaries Puzzle"

Instructions:

1. Introduce the activity page to your child.

2. Instruct your child to color and cut out each puzzle piece individually.

3. Write down a different scenario or action involving personal boundaries on each puzzle piece. For example, you could include scenarios like "Hugging a friend without permission" or "Sharing personal secrets."

4. Once all the puzzle pieces are ready, guide your child to solve the puzzle by connecting the pieces correctly. Encourage them to place the puzzle pieces in a way that respects personal boundaries.

5. As your child completes the puzzle, discuss each scenario together. Ask them why they placed each piece where they did and what it represents. Reinforce the idea that respecting personal boundaries and how their choices reflect that is important.

Respecting Boundaries Puzzle

Chapter 7: Creating and Cultivating Confidence

"Confidence is not about knowing everything, but trusting yourself enough to learn and grow from the unknown." - John Doe

Confidence is a child's development cornerstone, shaping how they navigate the world, interact with others, and achieve their goals. Building self-confidence begins early in life and is influenced by personality, experiences, and relationships with parents, peers, and other adults. Parents and caregivers can play a crucial role in fostering self-confidence in children, setting them up for success in their social, academic, and extracurricular pursuits.

Importance of Confidence

Confidence helps children navigate the world around them. It encourages them to explore, ask questions, and engage with their surroundings. It's the force that propels them to take risks, learn from their mistakes, and develop resilience. Children with high confidence levels are more likely to stand up for themselves, resist peer pressure, and exhibit a positive attitude toward learning and growth.

How to Cultivate Confidence in Children

1. Encourage Self-Expression

Allow children to express their thoughts, feelings, and ideas freely. This practice can foster a sense of self-assuredness and individuality. Encourage them to share their opinions and validate their feelings. By doing so, you reinforce their self-worth and build their confidence.

2. Foster Independence

Teach your children to do things for themselves. Assign age-appropriate tasks and responsibilities that they can complete independently. This autonomy can instill a sense of accomplishment and boost their confidence.

3. Provide Supportive Feedback

Feedback is a crucial component in the development of confidence. Positive reinforcement can help children understand their strengths, while constructive criticism can help them identify areas for improvement. Strive to provide balanced feedback that encourages growth and learning.

4. Encourage Perseverance

Instill the 'never give up' attitude in children. Teach them that it's okay to make mistakes and that failures are stepping stones to success. Encourage them to learn from their failures and keep trying until they succeed.

5. Nurture Interests

Identify and nurture your child's interests. Whether it's painting, dancing, science experiments, or soccer, encourage them to pursue activities they enjoy. This can help them develop skills, gain mastery, and build confidence.

6. Model Confidence

Children often emulate the behaviors they observe. Therefore, it's important for parents and caregivers to model confidence. Show them how you handle failures, take risks, and believe in your abilities.

Cultivating confidence in children is a continuous process that requires patience, love, and understanding. As parents, caregivers, and educators, it's our responsibility to create an environment that encourages children to believe in their abilities, express themselves freely, and develop resilience. With the right support and guidance, we can foster a generation of confident children ready to take on the world's challenges.

Remember, confidence is not about never failing but about getting back up each time we fall. It's about believing in oneself and possessing the courage to pursue one's dreams despite the odds. In the end, it's not just about creating confident children but about nurturing confident adults who can contribute positively to society.

Activities

Activity 70: My Body Is Amazing!

My Body Is Amazing

I AM SMART
I AM STRONG
I AM KIND
I AM ENOUGH
I AM GRATEFUL
I AM IMPORTANT
I AM LOVED

Instructions:

1. Print the coloring page and give it to your child.

2. Encourage your child to color in the outline of the body.

3. While they color, talk to them about the amazing things their body can do, such as running, jumping, or dancing.

4. Ask your child to think of one thing they love about their body and write it inside the outline.

5. Display the finished coloring page somewhere visible to remind your child of their uniqueness and the beauty of their body.

Embracing My Emotions

Embracing My Emotions

Instructions:

1. Print the emotional faces and speech bubbles provided.
2. Cut out the different emotional faces and speech bubbles.
3. Sit down with your child and explain that emotions are a normal part of life and embracing and expressing them is important.
4. Show your child the cutout emotion faces and ask them to identify each emotion.
5. Ask your child to choose an emotion face and place it on their face, role-playing that emotion.
6. Discuss situations that may cause different emotions and encourage your child to express their feelings.
7. Use the blank page for your child to draw their own emotions or create a story about different emotions using the cutouts.
8. Encourage your child to embrace and communicate their feelings openly.

Activity 72: Confidence Collage

Instructions:

1. Print the collage template and give your child-colored pencils, markers, or crayons.

2. Talk to your child about what confidence means and why feeling good about oneself is important.

3. Ask your child to think of positive qualities they possess or things they are proud of, such as kindness, creativity, or achievements.

4. Encourage your child to draw or write these positive qualities in the blank spaces of the collage template.

5. Help your child find photos of themselves engaging in activities they enjoy or accomplishing something they are proud of.

6. Cut out the photos and place them in the collage template, along with the positive words and drawings.

7. Display the completed collage in your child's room as a reminder of their strengths and accomplishments.

Celebrating Differences

Instructions:

1. Print the coloring page and give it to your child with colored pencils, markers, or crayons.

2. Sit down with your child and discuss how everyone is unique and special.

3. Ask your child to color in the diverse group of children on the coloring page, emphasizing the differences in hair color, skin tone, and clothing.

4. While coloring, discuss the importance of accepting and celebrating these differences.

5. Encourage your child to think of ways to show kindness and acceptance towards others who may be different.

6. Display the finished coloring page in a common area, such as the fridge, as a reminder of the value of diversity and acceptance.

Activity 74: Affirmation Booklet

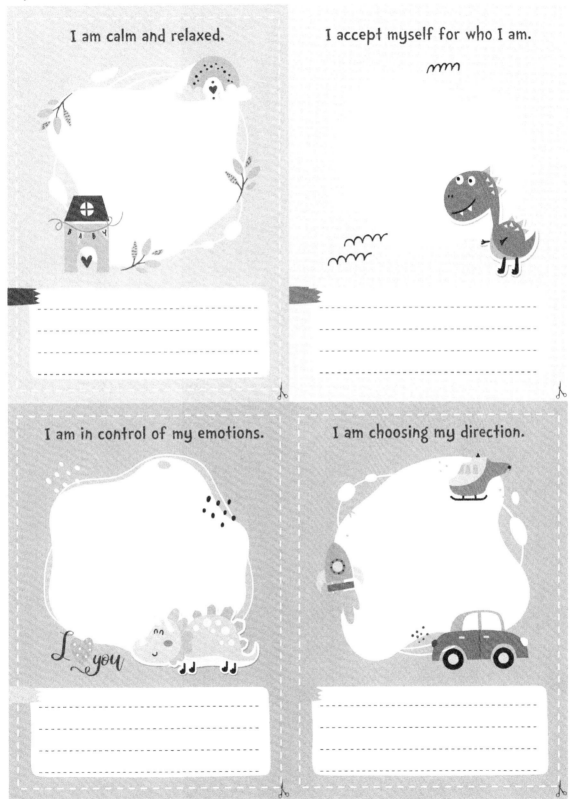

I am calm and relaxed.

I accept myself for who I am.

I am in control of my emotions.

I am choosing my direction.

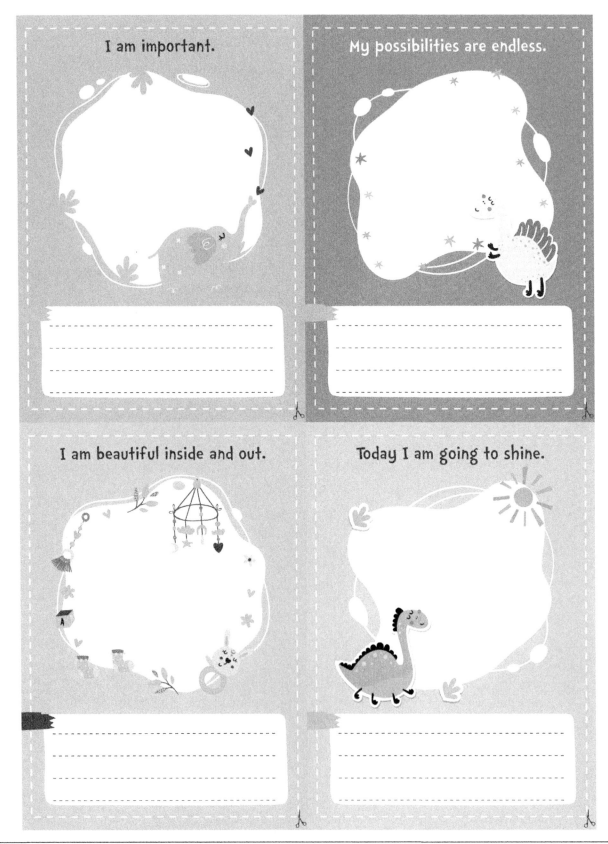

I am important.

My possibilities are endless.

I am beautiful inside and out.

Today I am going to shine.

I get better every single day.

My challenges help me grow.

My mistakes help me learn and grow.

I have courage and confidence.

Instructions:

1. Print the affirmation booklet and staple the pages together to form a booklet.

2. Sit down with your child and explain what affirmations are—positive statements that can boost self-confidence and self-esteem.

3. Read each affirmation in the booklet to your child and discuss its meaning.

4. Encourage your child to add illustrations or decorations to each page to make it personalized.

5. Each day, select one affirmation from the booklet and have your child read it aloud, repeating it a few times.

6. Discuss how the affirmation relates to your child's life.

7. Encourage your child to carry the booklet with them or place it somewhere they can easily access it whenever they need a confidence boost.

Instructions:

1. Print the mirror frame template and give your child colored pencils, markers, or crayons.
2. Talk to your child about the power of positive self-talk and how it can boost confidence.
3. Ask your child to look at themselves in a mirror and think about something they love or appreciate about themselves.
4. Encourage your child to draw or write their positive affirmation around the mirror frame.
5. Once they finish, invite your child to read the affirmation out loud while looking at themselves in the mirror.
6. Encourage your child to repeat this activity regularly, creating new affirmations or revisiting existing ones to reinforce positive self-perception.

Instructions:

1. Print the superhero templates and give your child coloring materials and scissors.
2. Discuss with your child the concept of inner strengths and superpowers they possess.
3. Ask your child to consider their strengths, such as kindness, courage, or creativity.
4. Encourage your child to write or draw their strengths and superpowers on the superhero templates.
5. Let your child color and decorate the superhero costumes and capes.
6. After they have completed their superhero creations, discuss how these strengths make them unique and powerful individuals.
7. Display the finished superheroes in your child's room as a reminder of their strengths and capabilities.

Embracing Mistakes

MISTAKES

Instructions:

1. Print the coloring page and give it to your child with colored pencils, markers, or crayons.

2. Talk to your child about the importance of embracing mistakes as learning opportunities.

3. Invite your child to color the word "Mistakes" using bright and vibrant colors.

4. Encourage your child to think about a recent mistake they made and discuss it together.

5. Ask your child to write or draw around the word "Mistakes" and what they learned or how they can grow from that experience.

6. Emphasize that mistakes are a natural part of learning and growth and should be celebrated for their efforts and ability to learn from them.

7. Display the finished coloring page as a reminder that mistakes are stepping stones to success.

Instructions:

1. Print the positive thought bubble template and give your child writing utensils.

2. Sit down with your child and explain the power of positive thoughts and how they can shape our self-perception.

3. Ask your child to think of positive thoughts or affirmations about themselves, such as "I am brave" or "I am kind."

4. Encourage your child to write or draw these positive thoughts within the thought bubbles on the template.

5. Remind your child to fill as many thought bubbles as possible with positive affirmations.

6. Encourage your child to keep the positive thought bubble template in a visible place, like their desk or bedroom, as a reminder of their inner strength and positivity.

Activity 78: Self-Appreciation Jar

Self-Appreciation Jar

Instructions:

1. Print the self-appreciation jar template and give your child colored pencils, markers, or crayons.

2. Talk to your child about the importance of self-appreciation and recognizing their achievements and positive qualities.

3. Ask your child to think of things they appreciate about themselves, such as acts of kindness or personal accomplishments.

4. Encourage your child to write or draw these positive aspects on the blank labels of the self-appreciation jar template.

5. Cut out the labels and help your child glue them onto the jar template, creating a collage of self-appreciation.

6. Display the completed self-appreciation jar in a visible place, such as their bedroom shelf.

7. Encourage your child to add more labels to the jar whenever they think of new things they appreciate about themselves, building a collection of self-love and self-esteem.

Chapter 8: Critical Thinking Exercises

"The essence of the independent mind lies not in what it thinks, but in how it thinks." – Christopher Hitchens.

Critical thinking is objectively analyzing, evaluating, and synthesizing information or ideas to make informed decisions or solve problems. It involves deep analysis, logical reasoning, and questioning assumptions and biases. Critical thinking can improve problem-solving, communication skills, and more effective decision-making.

The importance of critical thinking extends across all areas of life, including academics, work, and personal relationships. It enables individuals to approach situations with an open mind, consider different viewpoints, and develop well-reasoned conclusions. In today's world, where misinformation is prevalent, developing critical thinking skills is essential for uncovering the truth and making better choices.

Critical thinking is like being a detective for your thoughts and ideas. It means asking good questions, figuring out if something makes sense, and deciding if you agree or disagree with what you hear or see. When you use critical thinking, you're trying to find the best answers and make smart choices by thinking carefully and deeply about things. Critical thinking helps you be smarter, more curious, and better at solving problems.

Activities

Activity 79: "Mystery Maze"

It will help to develop deductive reasoning and problem-solving skills.

Instructions:

1. Hand out the "Mystery Maze" worksheet to your child.
2. Explain that they must help the character find the hidden treasure by solving the maze.
3. Encourage them to think critically and consider different paths before making a decision.
4. Remind them to use logical reasoning to eliminate incorrect options and choose the correct path.
5. Once they have solved the maze and found the treasure, they can color the worksheet to add a playful touch.

Mystery Maze

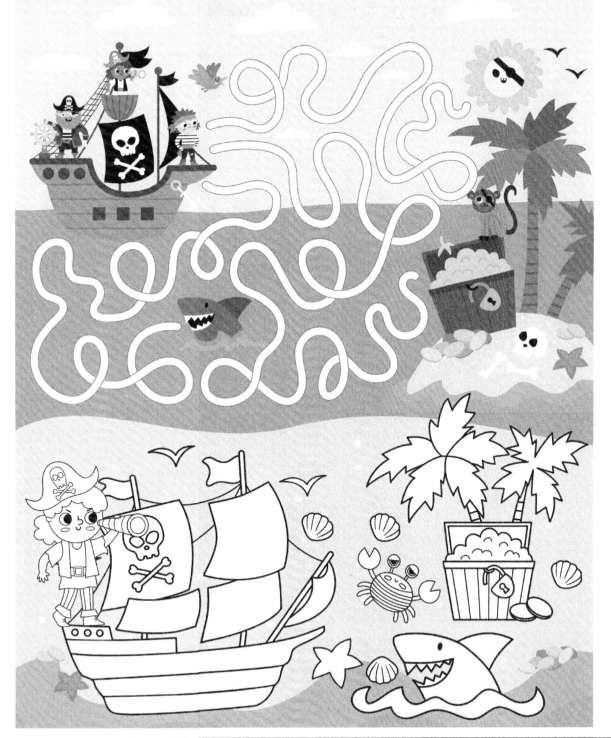

Activity 80: "Imagine It!"

This will help to enhance creative and hypothetical problem-solving skills.

Instructions:

1. Provide the "Imagine It!" worksheet to your child.
2. Ask them to imagine what life would be like if certain scenarios were true, such as living underwater or having superpowers.
3. Encourage them to think critically and develop creative solutions to their challenges in these scenarios.
4. Guide them to write or draw their ideas on the worksheet and let their imagination run wild.
5. After completing the worksheet, they can color the illustrations to add a playful element.

Imagine It!

Activity 81: "Puzzle Party"

It will strengthen problem-solving and analytical skills.

Instructions:

1. Provide the "Puzzle Party" worksheet to your child.
2. Explain that they must solve puzzles such as Sudoku, crosswords, or word search games.
3. Encourage them to think critically and analyze the clues or patterns to find the solutions.
4. Remind them to use logical reasoning and trial-and-error to tackle the puzzles.
5. After completing the puzzles, they can color the worksheet to make it more enjoyable.

Puzzle Party

Word search word list:
·Banana ·Mango ·Grapefruit ·Quince ·Apricot
·Raspberry ·Pineapple ·Melon ·Cranberry
·Cherry ·Lemon ·Peach ·Kiwi ·Pomelo ·Fig

1. TOOTH 2. HAIR 3. EYE 4. ARM 5. SHOULDER 6. ELBOW 7. FINGER 8. NECK 9. CHEEK
10. HAND 11. TONGUE 12. HEAD 13.EAR 14. PALM 15. EYEBROW 16 . FOREHEAD 17. NOSE

Activity 82: "Inventor's Workshop"

It will foster your child's creativity, problem-solving, and critical-thinking skills.

Instructions:

1. Hand out the "Inventor's Workshop" worksheet to your child.
2. Encourage them to imagine and design their invention to solve a specific problem or make life easier.
3. Ask them to think critically about how their invention works, what materials they need, and how it could benefit others.
4. Guide them to draw and describe their invention on the worksheet.
5. After completing the worksheet, they can color their invention and the workshop surroundings.

Inventor's Workshop

My Drawing

Activity 83: "Story Detectives"

This activity helps to develop critical thinking and analytical skills through storytelling.

Instructions:

1. Provide the "Story Detectives" worksheet to your child.
2. Ask them to read a short story or a passage and analyze it carefully.
3. Encourage them to think critically and answer the questions related to the story, such as identifying the main characters or predicting the ending.
4. Guide them to write or draw their responses on the worksheet.
5. After completing the activity, they can color the illustrations on the worksheet to add a playful touch.

Story Detectives

Once upon a time in a land of tall towers, there lived a brave knight named Sir Lionheart. He was a guardian of the magnificent castle.

Each day, Sir Lionheart stood strong near the castle gates. He was always ready to protect the castle and its people from any danger.

One day while Sir Lionheart was patrolling as usual along with his faithful horse Lightning, a dragon appeared and threatened the kingdom. He set out to face the beast.

It was a fierce battle, but in the end, Sir Lionheart was victorious and the dragon, instead of being defeated, became his friend.

 What was the knight's name?

Draw what the knight's sword might look like

What was the knight's duty?

Who was his faithful friend?

Activity 84: "Logic Builders"

This will strengthen logical reasoning and problem-solving skills.

Instructions:

1. Provide the "Logic Builders" worksheet to your child.
2. Explain that they need to solve a series of logical puzzles or riddles.
3. Encourage them to think critically and analyze the information to deduce the correct answers.
4. Guide them to write or draw their solutions on the worksheet.
5. After completing the activity, they can color the illustrations on the worksheet for a playful touch.

How Many?

Match the animals with their favorite food

Logic Builders

COLOR

1 blue 2 yellow 3 green 4 black

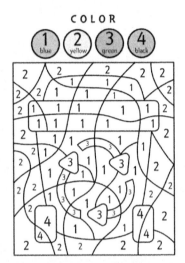

BIKE
CONTAINER
ELECTROCAR
FOREST
MOUNTAINS
PLANET
PLANT
SORTING
SUN
TREE

C	O	N	S	O	R	T	I
L	E	T	B	I	K	E	N
E	C	A	I	N	E	R	G
T	T	R	O	C	A	R	N
P	R	P	L	M	O	S	U
L	F	E	A	N	U	N	S
A	O	R	E	E	T	T	N
N	T	E	S	T	🌍	A	I

Spot 10 differences

Activity 85: "Creative Conundrums"

This will foster creative and critical thinking skills through problem-solving scenarios.

Instructions:

1. Hand out the "Creative Conundrums" worksheet to your child.
2. Present them with various hypothetical scenarios or problems.
3. Encourage them to think critically and develop creative solutions to solve the problems.
4. Guide them to write or draw their ideas on the worksheet.
5. After completing the activity, they can color the illustrations on the worksheet to make it more enjoyable.

Creative Conundrums

WHAT AM I?

I'm tropical and covered in spiky skin. Who am I?

I'm large, green on the outside, and red on the inside. Who am I?

I'm tropical and have a sweet, orange flesh. Who am I?

I'm sour and yellow, used to add flavor to dishes. Who am I?

I'm round and orange, often used to make juice. Who am I?

I'm small, brown, and have fuzzy skin. Who am I?

Find the correct shadow

SPOT 5 DIFFERENCES

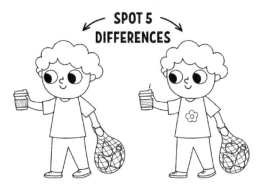

WORDSCRAMBLE

ROLAS NELAP

DWIN RUTBINE

NERTAICON

WORDSCRAMBLE

TENAPL

REET

PTANL

on

beside

above

in front of

on

between

near

behind

under

Activity 86: "Analytical Architects"

This will enhance analytical and critical thinking skills through building and design.

Instructions:

1. Provide the "Analytical Architects" worksheet to your child.
2. Ask them to design and draw their dream house or a unique structure.
3. Encourage them to think critically and consider various aspects such as functionality, aesthetics, and purpose.
4. Guide them to label and describe different design elements on the worksheet.
5. After completing the activity, they can color their architectural masterpiece and the surroundings.

Analytical Architects

My dream house

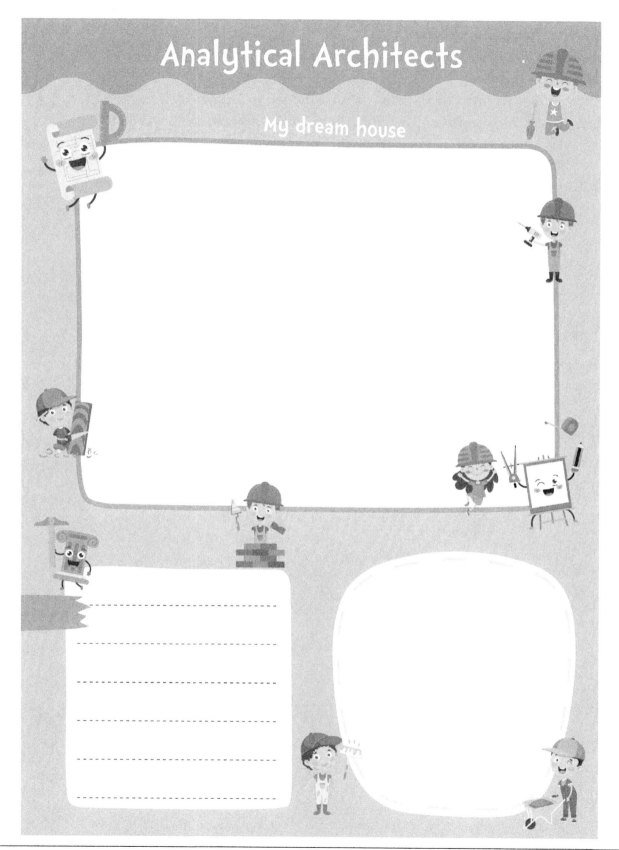

Activity 87: "Opinion Express"

Your child will develop critical thinking and communication skills through expressing opinions.

Instructions:

1. Hand out the "Opinion Express" worksheet to your child.
2. Present them with various topics or statements and ask them to form and express their opinions.
3. Encourage them to think critically and provide reasons to support their opinions.
4. Guide them to write or draw their opinions on the worksheet.
5. After completing the activity, they can color the illustrations on the worksheet for a playful touch.

Opinion Express

Are pets useful or helpful?

My opinions:

Are aliens real or fake?

Draw how you imagine an alien

Should mobile phones
be allowed in the classrooms?

My opinions:

Topics that interest me:

Activity 88: "Real-World Detectives"

It will help to enhance critical thinking and problem-solving skills through real-world scenarios.

Instructions:

1. Provide the "Real-World Detectives" worksheet to your child.
2. Present them with real-world scenarios or problems to analyze.
3. Encourage them to think critically and devise solutions or approaches to solve the problems.
4. Guide them to write or draw their ideas on the worksheet.
5. After completing the activity, they can color the illustrations on the worksheet to make it more enjoyable.

Real-World Detectives

 You wake up 15 minutes later than usual, it's an important day at school, you can't be late, What can you do?

 While you're in the middle of a test, the friend sitting behind you requests assistance. How might you respond?

 You used your sister's skates without permission, and they broke while you were using them. What actions could you take now?

 You haven't completed your homework, and your teacher is disappointed. What should you do?

Chapter 9: The Power of Mindfulness

"Mindfulness isn't difficult; we just need to remember to do it." – Sharon Salzberg

Mindfulness is an ancient practice that has gained significant attention in recent years for its effectiveness in promoting mental and emotional well-being. For children, practicing mindfulness can be particularly beneficial, allowing them to develop a greater awareness of their thoughts, feelings, and actions and to build essential life skills, such as emotional self-regulation, empathy, and resilience. Numerous theories and scientific studies support the importance of cultivating mindfulness in children, leading to a wide range of cognitive, emotional, and social benefits.

Mindfulness-Based Stress Reduction (MBSR) is one of the foundational theories explaining the mindfulness practice's efficacy. Developed by Dr. Jon Kabat-Zinn, MBSR emphasizes the role of mindfulness in reducing stress, anxiety, and depression. Children exposed to mindfulness through MBSR techniques develop a greater ability to focus, stay present and calm, manage their emotions, and handle stressful situations effectively.

Attachment Theory also supports the benefits of mindfulness for children. Children who experience secure attachments with their caregivers develop capacities for emotional regulation and empathy, which are both closely linked to mindfulness practice. By teaching children mindfulness techniques, parents and educators can help foster stronger attachment bonds, promoting the development of essential emotional and social competencies.

Benefits of Mindfulness for Children

Cognitive Benefits: Practicing mindfulness can lead to significant improvements in children's cognitive abilities, such as attention, memory, and executive function. Regular mindfulness practice has been shown to boost children's attention span, freeing them from distractions and enabling better focus on tasks. Mindfulness can also improve working memory and decision-making skills, which are vital for academic success.

Emotional Benefits: Mindfulness helps children recognize their emotions without judgment or resistance, enabling them to respond healthier and more adaptive. This emotional awareness fosters greater self-regulation and reduces impulsive reactions. As a result, children who practice mindfulness tend to experience reduced anxiety, stress, and depression and show increased resilience when faced with challenging situations.

Social Benefits: Developing mindfulness in children can lead to improved empathic skills and better relationships with peers and adults. As children learn to recognize and manage their own emotions through mindfulness, they become better equipped to understand and respond to the feelings of others. This empathic understanding results in stronger social connections, better communication skills, and a heightened awareness of the impact of their actions on others.

Activities

Activity 89: Guided Meditation

This guided meditation exercise is designed to help children (ages 6-12) develop mindfulness and imagination skills while incorporating playfulness into their daily routines.

Instructions:

1. Find a quiet, comfortable space where your child can sit or lie down without distractions.
2. Begin by explaining to your child that they are going on an imaginary adventure in their mind.
3. Ask them to relax, close their eyes, and take a few deep breaths.
4. Guide your child through a visualization using descriptive and engaging language. For example: "Imagine floating on a fluffy cloud high in the sky. The cloud gently carries you to a magical land filled with colorful flowers, talking animals, and sparkling waterfalls. As you explore this enchanting place, notice the sounds, smells, and sensations around you. Take your time to soak in the beauty and wonder of this imaginary adventure."
5. Allow your child to immerse themselves in their imagination and explore the imaginary world for a few minutes.
6. To conclude, gently bring your child's attention back to the present moment by asking them to wiggle their fingers and toes and slowly open their eyes.

Guided Meditation

Draw your favorite part of the imaginary adventure.

Write about one thing you saw, heard, or felt during the visualization.

How did you feel during the guided meditation?

Activity 90: The Taste Activity

- Give each child a raisin or a small piece of chocolate.
- Instruct them to hold the snack and not eat it yet. Have them close their eyes if that is comfortable.
- Guide the children through really focusing on the taste when they put the snack in their mouth. Encourage them to notice the flavors, textures, temperature, and even sounds of chewing.
- Remind them gently to return their attention to the taste when the mind wanders.
- After eating the snack, have the children discuss the experience. Talk about how mindfulness allows us to really savor and appreciate the taste of our food.

Activity 91: Sensory Awareness

This sensory awareness activity can be enjoyed by children (ages 3-6) and is particularly effective in helping them develop their senses and focus on the present moment.

Instructions:

1. Gather a collection of small objects with different textures, such as a soft toy, rough rock, smooth seashell, or bumpy fabric.
2. Sit with your child at a table or on the floor, placing the objects in front of both of you.
3. Explain that you will be exploring the textures of these objects using your sense of touch.
4. Encourage your child to pick up each object at a time and explore its texture by touching it with their fingers and hands.
5. As they touch each object, guide them to describe how it feels. For example, ask questions like: "Is it soft or rough?" "Does it feel warm or cool?" "What words would you use to describe the texture?"
6. Encourage your child to take time with each object and express their observations aloud.
7. Once they have explored all the objects, discuss their experiences and observations together.

Sensory Awareness

Draw your favorite object and describe its texture.

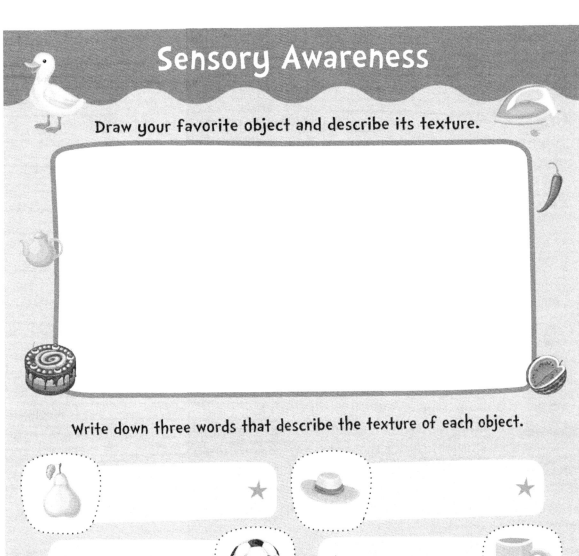

Write down three words that describe the texture of each object.

How did it feel to touch and explore the different textures?

Activity 92: Body Scan

Have the children sit or lie comfortably. Instruct them to close their eyes.

Guide them through a progressive relaxation exercise by focusing on different body parts one at a time:

- Toes - Encourage the children to curl and stretch their toes. Then, just focus on the feeling or sensation in their toes.
- Feet - Wiggle and relax their feet. Then, focus on any feelings, temperature, or tingling in their feet.
- Legs - Tell them to lightly tense and relax their leg muscles. Then, just observe any sensations in their legs.
- Stomach - Have them gently clench and release their stomach muscles. Then, focus on any feelings in their stomach area.
- Chest - Instruct them to take some deep breaths, bringing attention to their chest rising and falling.
- Arms - Tell them to flex and release their arms and then observe any sensations or feelings in their arms.
- Neck and shoulders - Have them shrug their shoulders and relax them. Focus on any tension or relaxation in this area.
- Face - Ask them to smile, frown, and relax their face. Then, observe how their face feels.
- Head - Tell them to gently move their head from side to side and relax and to notice any feelings in the head.
- Whole body - Ask the children to scan their whole body and notice any areas of tension. Encourage them to take a few deep breaths and relax their whole body.

Have the children open their eyes. Discuss how the exercise made them feel. Talk about how being mindful of our bodies can help us relax.

Activity 93: Mindful Breathing Practice

This mindful breathing exercise is suitable for children (ages 6-12) and teenagers (ages 13-18), promoting focus and calming the mind.

Instructions:

1. Sit with your child comfortably, ensuring they have a straight back and relaxed posture.
2. Explain that you will practice "Counting the Breath" together.
3. Instruct your child to take a slow, deep breath in through their nose, counting silently to themselves as they do so.
4. As they exhale through their mouth, guide them to count silently again, matching the length of their inhale.
5. Encourage your child to continue consistently counting their breaths, inhaling, and exhaling.
6. If their mind wanders, gently remind them to bring their attention back to the counting and the sensation of their breath.

7. Practice this breathing exercise for a few minutes, allowing your child to develop a sense of calm and focus.

• Write down the highest number you reached while counting your breaths.

_____

• How did your mind and body feel after practicing this breathing exercise?

_____

_____

_____

Activity 94: The Color Wheel

1. Gather coloring supplies like crayons, markers, and colored pencils.
2. Have the children sit comfortably with a blank piece of paper in front of them.
3. Instruct them to choose a color and start coloring any part of the page. Encourage them to choose colors at random and switch colors when they feel like it.
4. Guide them to color mindfully - really focusing on the color, shape, texture, and movement of the crayon or pencil.
5. Remind them gently to return their focus to coloring when the mind wanders.
6. After 5-10 minutes, have the children stop coloring. Ask them to observe their artwork without judgment. Just notice the patterns, shapes, and colors on the page.
7. Discuss how mindfulness of coloring allows us to enjoy the process without worrying about the outcome. Talk about how our brains need restful activities like this.

Activity 95: Guided Visualization

This guided visualization exercise is suitable for children (ages 6-12) and can spark imagination and relaxation.

Instructions:

1. Find a quiet, comfortable space where your child can sit or lie down without distractions.
2. Explain that you will take them on a journey to "The Secret Garden" through their imagination.
3. Ask your child to close their eyes and take a few deep breaths to help them relax.
4. Guide them through a visualization using descriptive and engaging language. For example: "Imagine standing before a big, wooden gate. Slowly open the gate and step into "The Secret Garden." As you enter, notice the vibrant colors of flowers, the scent of blooming petals, and the gentle warmth of the sun on your skin. Explore this magical garden, discovering hidden paths, sparkling fountains, and friendly creatures. Take your time to absorb the beauty and tranquility of this special place."
5. Encourage your child to use all their senses to immerse themselves in the visualization.
6. After a few minutes, gently guide them to the present moment by asking them to wiggle their fingers and toes and slowly open their eyes.

Guided Visualization

Draw your favorite flower you encountered in the visualization.

Write about one thing you saw, smelled, or felt in 'The Secret Garden.'

How did you feel during the guided visualization?

Activity 96: Mindful Breathing Practice

This playful, mindful breathing exercise is suitable for younger children (ages 3-6) and helps them develop focus and deep breathing techniques.

Instructions:

1. Sit with your child in a comfortable position, either on the floor or in chairs.
2. Explain that you will practice "Bubble Breath" together, imagining blowing bubbles.
3. Demonstrate taking a deep breath through your nose, and as you exhale through your mouth, pretend to blow a big imaginary bubble.
4. Encourage your child to mimic your actions, taking a deep breath and blowing out like a bubble.
5. Practice this breathing exercise, making it playful by pretending to blow bubbles of different sizes or colors with each exhale.
6. Encourage your child to focus on their breath and enjoy the playful sensation of blowing bubbles.

• Draw a picture of a bubble you blew during the exercise.

• Describe how it felt to take deep breaths and blow imaginary bubbles.

_____

_____

_____

• How did your body and mind feel after practicing "Bubble Breath"?

_____

_____

_____

Activity 97: Sensory Awareness Activity

This sensory awareness activity is suitable for children (ages 6-12) and encourages them to engage their five senses while exploring their surroundings.

Instructions:

1. Explain to your child that you will go on a "Five Senses Scavenger Hunt" to explore the world around you.

2. Provide a list of items or sensations to find or observe that engage each of the five senses: sight, hearing, touch, smell, and taste.

3. Go for a walk together or explore your home while encouraging your child to pay attention to the items or sensations on the list.

4. As your child finds or experiences each item, discuss and reflect on their observations, helping them deepen their sensory awareness.

5. Encourage your child to describe what they see, hear, touch, smell, and taste in detail, fostering mindfulness of their surroundings.

Sensory Awareness Activity

Sight:
Draw or write about something beautiful you saw during the scavenger hunt.

Hearing:
Describe a sound you heard that caught your attention.

Touch:
Draw or describe something you touched and how it felt.

Smell:
Write down a scent that stood out during the activity.

Taste:
Share a taste experience you had during the scavenger hunt.

Activity 98: The Leaf Rubbing Activity

Materials needed:

- Large leaves (2-3 per child)
- Paper
- Crayons (at least 2-3 colors per child)

Instructions:

1. Have the children sit in a circle or gather around a table. Give each child 2-3 large leaves and a couple of sheets of paper.

2. Say: "Today, we are going to do an activity called leaf rubbing. We will use crayons and leaves to create art."

3. Demonstrate how to do a leaf rubbing:
   - Place the leaf vein-side down on the paper
   - Put a crayon underneath the leaf
   - Rub the side of the crayon over the leaf to make an imprint on the paper

4. Guide the children to choose a crayon color and start rubbing their first leaf mindfully:
   - Instruct them to pay close attention to the texture and veins of the leaf
   - Encourage them to notice how much or how little pressure is needed
   - Remind them to focus on the physical sensations in their hands
   - Guide them to return their focus to the activity when the mind wanders

5. As the children work, watch for signs that their attention is drifting. Gently guide them back to focusing on the following:
   - The color they chose
   - The texture of the leaf under their crayon
   - The movement of their hand
   - The sound the crayon makes

6. When they are finished, have the children observe their leaf rubbings without judgment. Guide them to simply notice:
   - The different lines and patterns
   - How the colors blended together
   - The unique shape of each leaf rubbing

Lead a discussion on how focusing the senses on everyday activities helps develop mindfulness. The children can take their leaf rubbings home to share with family.

Activity 99: Mindful Breathing Balloon

Mindful Breathing Balloon

This playful activity will help your child practice mindfulness through deep breathing. Follow these steps together:

1. Print this page and encourage your child to color and decorate the balloon. They can use their favorite colors and be as creative as they like!

2. Once the balloon is colored, help your child carefully cut it out along the dotted line.

3. Find a quiet and comfortable space. Guide your child to sit down and hold the balloon in their hands.

4. Instruct your child to take a deep breath through their nose while slowly inflating the balloon by expanding their belly. Count to three as they fill the balloon with air.

5. Encourage your child to pause for a moment, noticing how it feels to have a full balloon.

6. Then, ask them to exhale slowly through their mouth, deflating the balloon while counting to three. They should feel their bellies contracting as the air leaves the balloon.

7. Repeat this breathing exercise a few times, allowing your child to focus on their breath and the sensations it brings.

Remember to emphasize the importance of taking slow and deep breaths, just like inflating and deflating a balloon. This activity can be a fun way for your child to learn how to calm their mind and be present in the moment.

Enjoy this mindful adventure with your little one!

Activity 100: Sensory Nature Walk

Materials needed:

- Music (optional)
- Space to move around

Instructions:

1. Have the children spread out so each has enough space to move freely.
2. Say: "Today, we are going to move our bodies mindfully. We will focus all our attention on how our bodies feel as we move in different ways."
3. Guide the children through a series of movements, instructing them to focus on:
   - The feeling of their feet on the floor
   - The sensations in their muscles as they move
   - The changes in breathing as they move faster or slower
   - Any sounds their bodies make
4. Give simple movement instructions:
   - Walk around the room slowly, paying attention to each step
   - March on the spot, noticing how your legs and arms move together
   - Stretch your arms up high, focusing on the feelings in your shoulders and back
   - Spin in a circle, concentrating on the sensations in your body
5. If using music, raise and lower the tempo to encourage faster and slower movements.
6. Gently guide the children to return their focus to how their body feels when their attention wanders.
7. When the activity ends, have the children stand still and close their eyes. Guide them through 'scanning' their bodies from head to toe, noticing any areas that feel warm, tingly, or relaxed.

Mindful Sensory Playdough

This hands-on activity will allow them to enjoy the calming benefits of tactile stimulation and unleash their creativity. Let's get started:

1. Print the two pages and encourage your child to color and decorate the playdough shape. They can use vibrant colors to make it visually appealing and enticing.

2. Once the playdough shape is colored, provide your child with the cutout sensory elements such as dots, stripes, stars, or any other shapes that can enhance the sensory experience. These can be printed or cut from magazines or colored paper.

3. Guide your child to color and decorate the sensory elements as they wish. They can use different colors, patterns, or textures to make them visually interesting and engaging.

4. Encourage your child to imagine the sensations they would like to experience with their playdough. They can think about scents, textures, or even sounds that they would like to associate with their playdough creation.

5. Help your child make homemade scented playdough by following a simple recipe together. You can find many playdough recipes online that use common household ingredients. Add a few drops of essential oils or natural scents to create a delightful aroma.

6. Once the playdough is ready, invite your child to shape and mold it using the sensory elements they decorated earlier. Encourage them to explore the different textures, experiment with different shapes, and enjoy the therapeutic benefits of manipulating the play dough.

7. As your child engages in sensory playdough, encourage them to focus on the present moment, noticing the sensations, scents, and textures they experience. Encourage them to take deep breaths and enjoy the calming effects of the activity.

This activity will provide your child with a mindful and sensory-rich experience, allowing them to relax, explore their creativity, and focus on the present moment. It's a delightful way to engage their senses and promote mindfulness through play.

Chapter 10: A Sense of Community: Working Towards Positive Habits

Parents and caregivers play a crucial role in promoting positive behaviors by influencing their child's behavior through parenting knowledge, attitudes, and practices and fostering learning motivation.

The Impact of Parenting Knowledge, Attitudes, and Practices

Parenting knowledge, attitudes, and practices are crucial in shaping children's social, emotional, and intellectual development. When parents are equipped with the right information and adopt positive parenting techniques like an authoritative parenting style, they are better able to create an environment that nurtures a sense of community among their children.

In addition to understanding child development theories and best practices concerning discipline strategies as part of building positive habits within the family unit or community setting, caregivers themselves need to practice self-reflection regarding personal beliefs about what makes effective parent-child relationships work smoothly over time without any negative impacts on various aspects such as strengthening families or preventing adverse outcomes.

How Parents Can Influence Their Child's Behavior

Parents and caregivers hold significant power in shaping their children's behavior through various means, such as emotional regulation, positive reinforcement, and effective discipline strategies.

Being attentive to your child's needs, consistently enforcing rules, and providing clear expectations can greatly impact how children learn and develop good habits.

In addition to cultivating positive actions through encouragement and rewards, parents should also be mindful of how they display emotions. Children often look up to adults as role models who set the tone for acceptable behavior within family dynamics.

By demonstrating appropriate emotional responses and proper coping mechanisms during challenging situations, parents can teach children invaluable lessons that will serve them well later in life.

This includes setting cultural norms that influence how children relate with others while incorporating elements from varying disciplines of child psychology into everyday practices.

The Role of Motivation in Learning

Understanding the role of motivation in learning is crucial for parents and caregivers who want to help their children develop positive habits. Motivation is significant in a child's willingness to engage with new tasks, learn from mistakes, and persist through challenges.

There are two main types of motivation: intrinsic and extrinsic. Intrinsic motivation comes from within the individual, driven by personal interests, passion, or enjoyment related to the task at hand.

Externally motivated individuals may need rewards or recognition outside of themselves as they strive for achievements guided by external factors such as praise or competitive pressures.

Fostering a sense of community and working together to build positive habits will enhance student motivation on multiple levels. By involving families in educational activities and decision-making processes (family involvement), we create stronger connections between home life and school experiences. This partnership reinforces academic success while cultivating emotional well-being throughout childhood development stages.

The Benefits of Building Positive Habits in a Group Setting

Building positive habits in a group setting fosters new positive behaviors and friendships through teamwork – and collaboration increases motivation and accountability in social settings and makes activities more fun and engaging.

Foster New Positive Habits and Friendships through Teamwork and Collaboration

Collaboration and teamwork are crucial in developing positive habits and fostering new friendships in children. Here are some ways parents and caregivers can encourage teamwork and collaboration:

1. **Encourage group activities that require cooperation:** Participating in group activities, such as sports or team-building exercises, can help children learn the importance of working with others towards a common goal.

2. **Highlight the benefits of mutual aid:** Teach children how helping others can be rewarding for everyone involved and lead to more effective problem-solving.

3. **Model healthy communication skills:** By modeling active listening, respect for others' opinions, and clear communication, parents can encourage children to communicate effectively with their peers.

4. **Facilitate opportunities for relationship building:** Providing opportunities for children to interact with others in different settings outside of school or extracurricular activities can foster new friendships and broaden social horizons.

5. **Celebrate progress together:** Recognize achievements made by a group effort to reinforce the importance of collaboration in achieving goals.

By encouraging teamwork among children in various settings, parents can help them build relationships and develop positive habits that will benefit them long-term.

Increase Motivation and Accountability in Social Settings

Building positive habits in a group setting can be instrumental in increasing motivation and accountability, especially for children. Working out with friends or participating in group activities can create a sense of accountability as everyone works towards the same goal.

This kind of team effort also fosters motivation as each participant feeds off the energy and enthusiasm of others.

Tracking progress toward building positive habits in a social setting creates a sense of ownership over individual actions and encourages individuals to take responsibility for their progress.

Children who track their performance alongside peers are more likely to feel motivated to improve, which leads them toward greater accountability.

Make Activities More Fun and Engaging

Building positive habits in a group setting can make activities more fun and engaging for children. When working towards healthy lifestyle habits, like exercise or healthy eating, it can be challenging to motivate kids to participate.

For example, creating a walking club with other parents and their children or organizing healthy cooking classes where kids work together to prepare meals encourages teamwork and collaboration while making these activities enjoyable.

Encouraging Community Involvement and Collaboration

Suggest ways for parents to get other parents and children involved, learn, and work together as a team to benefit everyone, building a sense of community and support.

Suggesting Ways for Parents to Get Other Parents and Children Involved

Promoting positive habits in your child and encouraging community involvement and collaboration is important as a parent or caregiver. Here are some ways you can do that:

1. **Organize group activities and events:** Plan events like picnics, game nights, or movie screenings where families can spend quality time together.
2. **Create a supportive social media group:** Use social media platforms like Facebook or WhatsApp to create a group where parents can share ideas, ask questions, and stay connected.
3. **Collaborate with schools and community organizations:** Partner with your child's school or local nonprofits to organize volunteer opportunities or joint community projects.
4. **Encourage regular check-ins and accountability:** Schedule regular meetings or check-ins with other parents to discuss progress on building positive habits and hold each other accountable.

Engaging in these activities can help foster a sense of community among parents and children. Working together towards common goals can also increase accountability, motivation, and success in building positive habits.

Learning and Working Together for the Benefit of Everyone

Encouraging community involvement and collaboration is key to building positive habits for children. When parents, caregivers, and children work together towards a common goal, they can achieve more than they would individually.

This creates an environment where everyone's strengths benefit the team or group.

In addition to strengthening relationships between community members, collaborative teamwork can promote innovation and find solutions to resolve problems that may arise.

By working together, parents and children can learn from each other while fostering a sense of belonging and shared responsibility.

Building a Sense Of Community and Support

Building a sense of community and support is vital for helping children develop positive habits at home and in their wider social circles. When parents work together to encourage good behavior, they create a supportive environment that fosters healthy growth and development.

Families can share resources, ideas, and experiences through these partnerships to build stronger relationships. This helps everyone involved feel more connected to their peers while learning valuable lessons about effective communication, problem-solving strategies, and conflict-resolution techniques.

Coming together as a team committed to promoting positive behaviors within their communities makes it easier for parents to provide the guidance and structure needed for children's success.

Strategies for Involving Other Parents and Children

Organize group activities and events to encourage participation, create a supportive social media group for ongoing communication, collaborate with schools and community organizations for larger-scale initiatives, and encourage regular check-ins and accountability.

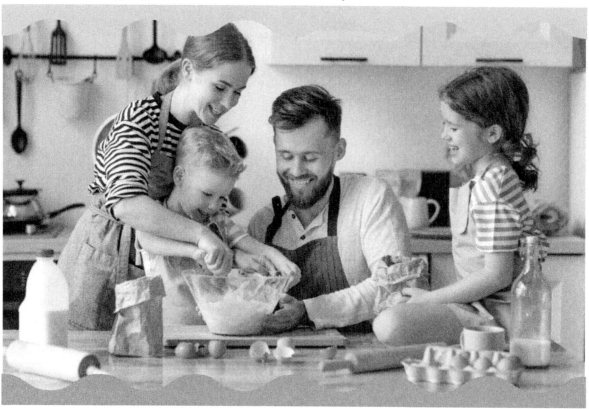

Organizing Group Activities and Events

Organizing group activities and events is a great way to build positive habits in children and foster a sense of community. Here are some strategies for involving other parents and children:

1. Consider hosting a family-friendly fitness event like a fun run or bike ride.
2. Plan a neighborhood clean-up day where families can work together to beautify their community.

3. Organize a community service project, like volunteering at a food bank or nursing home.

4. Host a book club or reading circle for kids and parents to discuss literature.

5. Schedule regular playdates or sports games to encourage teamwork and collaboration among children.

6. Consider organizing joint field trips to museums, parks, or local attractions with other families.

7. Create a Facebook group for parents to share ideas and plan activities together.

By collaborating with others in the community and engaging in group activities, children can learn valuable social skills and develop positive habits for life.

Creating a Supportive Social Media Group

Creating a supportive social media group can be an excellent tool for building community and promoting positive habits among children. The group can allow parents and caregivers to connect and share tips, strategies, and ideas about parenting in the digital age.

When designing this supportive network on social media, it's important to focus on literacy in several areas, such as online safety, digital citizenship, and mental health awareness.

This platform enables parents and other caregivers to share information that helps them stay informed about trends or challenges they may face when raising their children in our modern era.

Parents could also encourage active participation by planning virtual and physical events for the kids while exercising caution when necessary.

Collaborating with Schools and Community Organizations

Collaborating with schools and community organizations is a key component in building positive habits in children. By working together, parents and caregivers can create a supportive environment that encourages healthy behaviors and well-being.

This can include participating in volunteer activities, attending parent education classes, and developing two-way communication channels between schools and families. When educators and parents work as partners, they provide important opportunities for children to develop social skills, emotional intelligence, and academic competencies.

Encouraging Regular Check-ins and Accountability

Regular check-ins and accountability are crucial for building community and working towards positive habits. By checking in with each other regularly, parents and caregivers can stay on track with their goals for themselves, their children, and the larger community.

One effective way to encourage regular check-ins is by creating a support system or network of like-minded individuals who share similar values and goals. This could be done by joining a parent-teacher association (PTA), attending local school board meetings, or even forming a social media group where everyone can communicate regularly.

Overcoming Challenges and Obstacles

We'll explore common challenges and barriers that may arise while building positive habits in a community, offering solutions to help you tackle them head-on.

Addressing Resistance to Change and Setbacks

As parents and caregivers, it's important to acknowledge that building positive habits in a community setting can be challenging. Resistance to change and setbacks are common obstacles that must be addressed for success.

Specific strategies have been proven effective in helping organizations overcome unproductive resistance to change, such as getting people involved in making the change or providing additional resources and training.

Additionally, building resilience is important for bouncing back from setbacks and enduring hardship. Promoting adaptability, perseverance, flexibility, innovation, growth mindset, and problem-solving skills among children at an early age in a supportive community setting with other parents/caregivers can go a long way toward overcoming obstacles together.

Assessing Progress and Celebrating Success

Track your progress and celebrate every achievement, no matter how small. In this blog post, you'll discover effective strategies for building positive habits in a community setting.

Setting Goals and Tracking Progress

To successfully build positive habits in a community setting, it is important to set specific, measurable goals and track progress toward achieving them. This means identifying the long-term objectives and breaking them down into smaller, achievable steps.

By doing so, parents and caregivers can help children develop planning, decision-making, and self-reflection skills.

For example, if the goal is for a child to read more books this year than last year. A SMART objective would be for the child to read one book weekly over three months by allocating 15 minutes of reading time each day.

Recognizing and Celebrating Milestones and Achievements

Recognizing and celebrating milestones and achievements is important to building positive habits within a community. Here are some ways parents and caregivers can encourage this in their children:

1. **Acknowledge progress:** Take the time to acknowledge small steps towards a goal, such as completing homework on time or practicing a new skill.

2. **Celebrate accomplishments:** When a child achieves something significant, celebrate it! This could be as simple as baking their favorite treat or planning a special outing.

3. **Boost confidence:** Recognizing achievements can boost confidence and encourage children to continue working towards their goals.

4. **Commemorate successes:** Consider creating a physical reminder of achievement, such as framing artwork or displaying a trophy.

5. **Provide recognition:** Publicly acknowledging achievements, whether it's through social media or at a family gathering, can provide an additional sense of accomplishment.

6. **Celebrate success at work:** If both parents work outside the home, they should celebrate each other's wins. This will enhance their engagement with work and improve job satisfaction.

7. **Encourage healthy competition:** Earning rewards for reaching goals is an excellent way to motivate children to develop healthy habits while encouraging competition between group friends.

8. **Emphasize teamwork:** Finally, remember that recognizing and celebrating milestones is not just about individual accomplishments but also about teamwork and collaboration within the community and among teammates in sports groups or clubs where kids may be involved.

By taking the time to recognize and celebrate even small achievements along the way, parents and caregivers can help children build positive habits that will serve them well throughout their lives.

Providing Positive Feedback and Reinforcement

Recognizing and celebrating small successes is essential when working towards positive habits in a community setting. Positive feedback and reinforcement are critical in motivating and connecting people towards a sense of community.

Appreciation, coaching, and evaluation are three forms of feedback that can be used to promote positive behaviors. For example, praising a child for completing their homework on time or cheering them on during a sports game can boost their self-esteem and encourage them to keep working towards their goals.

Building Positive Habits takes constant practice, dedication, and commitment from children and parents/caregivers.

Moving Forward In Building Positive Habits

To continue building positive habits within a community, it's important to encourage ongoing learning and growth, emphasize the importance of support from others, and provide actionable steps and resources for continued success.

Encouraging Ongoing Learning and Growth

Parents and caregivers must encourage ongoing learning and growth to instill lifelong learning habits in children. This involves creating an environment that fosters curiosity, exploration, and self-discovery.

One way to do this is by providing opportunities for children to learn new things regularly.

It's also essential to emphasize the importance of continuous improvement and personal development as they grow up. Children should be encouraged to take responsibility for their learning by setting goals, monitoring progress, and celebrating achievements.

Parents can model a growth mindset by sharing stories of overcoming challenges through perseverance and hard work.

Emphasizing the Importance of Community Support

A sense of community support can play a critical role in developing positive habits among children and caregivers. With support from others, we tend to feel more motivated, accountable, and connected - all of which are key factors that help build long-lasting healthy habits.

As parents or caregivers, when you encourage social involvement within your community, you can provide opportunities for teamwork and collaboration toward shared goals.

Being part of a positive community comes with many benefits, including improved mental health and physical health outcomes and cultivating a greater understanding of kindness and inclusivity among members.

Some research studies have found that individuals who experience social isolation may be at an increased risk for health challenges such as depression or high blood pressure.

Building relationships with others provides us with emotional support during difficult times, allowing us to weather life's ups and downs more successfully.

Conclusion

We have embarked on a journey of nurturing and guiding the next generation toward a brighter future. Throughout this book, we have explored a wide range of activities designed to cultivate positive behavior in children, promoting kindness, empathy, social skills, and good habits.

As parents, caregivers, educators, and mentors, we play a crucial role in shaping the character and values of our children. It is our responsibility to instill in them the importance of treating others with respect, showing empathy towards those in need, and embracing good habits that will pave the way for a successful and fulfilling life. "Positive Behavior Activities for Kids" offers a treasure trove of ideas and strategies to help us in this noble endeavor.

We have learned that children are like sponges, eagerly absorbing the world around them and imitating the behaviors they witness. By providing them with a variety of engaging and enjoyable activities, we can create an environment that fosters positive behavior and personal growth. From group games that promote teamwork and cooperation to solo exercises that encourage self-reflection and mindfulness, each activity in this book has been carefully selected to empower children with the tools they need to navigate the challenges of life with confidence and integrity.

Furthermore, we have discovered the significance of modeling positive behavior ourselves. Children learn best by observing and emulating those around them, so we must lead by example. By demonstrating kindness, empathy, and good habits in our own lives, we inspire children to do the same. The activities in this book serve as valuable learning experiences and opportunities for us to connect with children, share our wisdom, and reinforce the values we hold dear.

"Positive Behavior Activities for Kids" is not just a collection of games and exercises but a roadmap to building a brighter and more compassionate world. By instilling kindness, empathy, social skills, and good habits in our children, we empower them to become responsible citizens who positively impact their communities. We are creating a ripple effect that will extend far beyond the pages of this book as these children grow into compassionate adults who continue to spread love, acceptance, and positivity wherever they go.

As we conclude this journey, let us remember that shaping the behavior and character of children is an ongoing process. It requires dedication, patience, and a commitment to continuous learning. The activities presented in this book are just the beginning—an invitation to explore, adapt, and expand upon them according to the unique needs and interests of the children in our care.

Check out another book in the series

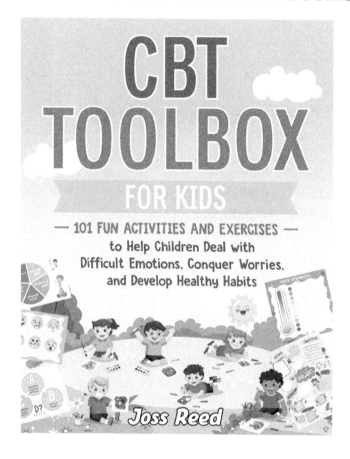

References

Bledsoe, J. (2014, January 3). 101-weekend family activity ideas. All Pro Dad. https://www.allprodad.com/101-weekend-family-activity-ideas/

Daniel, P. (2017). Importance of Family Bonding, 6 Family Bonding activities and games at home | ParentCircle. https://www.parentcircle.com/importance-of-family-bonding-activities-and-games/article

Eatough, E. (n.d.). 20 family tradition ideas to strengthen bonds and make memories. Betterup.com. https://www.betterup.com/blog/family-traditions

Hochswender, C. (2015, July 14). 20 fun family weekend activities to do at home. Parents. https://www.parents.com/fun/activities/outdoor/weekend-family-activities/

Schuman, C. (2015, July 14). 10 unique family activities to do with your kids. Parents. https://www.parents.com/fun/activities/unique-family-activities/

Stephanie. (2022, March 2). Why family bonding is more important now than ever before. Let's Roam Explorer. https://www.letsroam.com/explorer/family-bonding/

Thakur, S. (2020, July 7). 10 ways to create family bonding and its importance. MomJunction. https://www.momjunction.com/articles/family-bonding_00633863/

Today's Parent. (2020, November 18). 87 fun things to do at home— avoid that coronavirus cabin fever - Today's Parent. Today's Parent: SJC Media. https://www.todaysparent.com/family/activities/fun-things-to-do-at-home/

Witmer, D. (2008, September 24). How to strengthen family bonds. Verywell Family. https://www.verywellfamily.com/how-to-strengthen-your-familys-bond-ten-tips-2609591

Alanen L (2009) Johdatus lapsuudentutkimukseen [Introduction to childhood studies]. In: Alanen L and Karila K (eds) Lapsuus, lapsuuden instituutiot ja lasten toiminta. Tampere: Vastapaino, pp. 9–30

Andresen A, Garðarsdóttir O, Janfelt M, et al. (2011) Barnen och välfärdspolitiken: nordiska barndomar 1900-2000 [Children and welfare policy: Nordic childhoods 1900-2000]. Stockholm: Dialogos

Berg P and Peltola M (2015) Raising decent citizens – On respectability, parenthood and drawing boundaries. NORA – Nordic Journal of Feminist and Gender Research 23(1): 36–51.

Elvstrand H and Närvänen AL (2016) Children's own perspectives on participation in leisure-time centers in Sweden. American Journal of Educational Research 4(6): 496–503.

Finnish National Board of Education (FNBE) (2011) Perusopetuksen aamu- ja iltapäivätoiminnan perusteet [The national core curriculum for before- and after-school activities for schoolchildren].

Finnish National Board of Education (FNBE) (2014) Perusopetuksen opetussuunnitelman perusteet [National core curriculum for basic education]. Available at: https://www.oph.fi/sites/default/files/documents/perusopetuksen_opetussuunnitelman_perusteet_2014.pdf (accessed 2 April 2020).

Haglund B (2015) Pupils' opportunities to influence activities: A study of everyday practice at a Swedish leisure-time center. Early Child Development and Care 185(10): 1556–1568. Haglund B and Anderson S (2009) Afterschool programs and leisure-time centers: Arenas for learning and leisure. World Leisure Journal 51(2): 116–129https://www.amazon.com/dp/B0979CN1YX

Printed in Great Britain
by Amazon